BibleStudy.Tips

BibleStudy.Tips
Learn to Navigate God's Word

LaRosa M. Johnson, Jr.

Urban Scholar Books
Jacksonville, NC

Bible Study Tips: Learn to Navigate God's Word

Copyright © 2021 by LaRosa Johnson, revised October 2021

Published by Urban Scholar Books
urbanscholarbooks.com

All rights reserved. No part of this publication may be reproduced, stored in a retrieval system or transmitted in any form by any means, electronic, mechanical, photocopy, recording or otherwise, without the prior permission of the publisher, except as provided by USA copyright law.

Cover design: LaRosa Johnson

Unless otherwise noted, all Scripture quotations are taken from the Christian Standard Bible®, Copyright © 2017 by Holman Bible Publishers. Used by permission. Christian Standard Bible® and CSB® are federally registered trademarks of Holman Bible Publishers.

ISBN (print): 978-0-9963233-2-1
ISBN (ebook): 978-0-9963233-3-8

This book is dedicated to the Church, Christ's bride.
I pray this workbook helps you:
Learn the Bible
Connect with God
Grow in your faith

I also dedicate this to my children.
I pray you use this workbook to learn about the Faith
& experience the truth of the gospel for yourselves.

Contents

Preface ix

How to Use This Workbook xi

Bible Study Tips

Week 1: Bible Journaling 1

Week 2: Cross-Reference Study 23

Week 3: Bible Survey Study 43

Week 4: Topical Study 65

Week 5: Character Study 89

Week 6: Word Study 111

Weeks 7&8: Inductive Bible Study 135

Appendices

Appendix 1: 5 Things to Pray Before You Study 176

Appendix 2: How to Build a Bible Study Library 180

Appendix 3: How to Pick the Perfect Study Bible 184

Appendix 4: Biblical Meditation 190

Appendix 5: Additional Passages for Study 194

Appendix 6: Foundations 260 Bible Reading Plan 196

Leader's Guide & Bonus Content 204

Preface

There are few things that are as encouraging to a pastor as when a member of his flock loves the Word of God and grows in his or her proficiency in studying the Word. Such a member not only encourages their pastor but spurs their pastor on to continue to grow in his own study of the Bible. What you hold in your hand is the fruit of such love and hard work of one of my former members of our church, LaRosa Johnson.

Bible study is always fruitful for the one who is willing to put in the time and effort; but, as LaRosa makes clear, it is hard. It is not hard in the sense that it is hard to understand. Rather, one reason I believe it is hard is because of the countless other distractions and little time stealers we have in our lives that rob us of such a precious commodity: our time. But it is also hard for those who do not know where to start or do not know of the basic tools they have at their disposal that will help them reap a harvest from their Bible study after spending time doing the work in the soil of the Scriptures.

What is so wonderful about this workbook, beyond all of the helpful tips, tools, and practice that fill its pages, is the fact that LaRosa does not write as a pastor, scholar, or theologian, though he is capable and more in each arena. Instead, he writes with a heart for others to grow in their love for and ability (and fruitfulness) in studying God's Word. It is one of the things that has drawn my affections for LaRosa. And it is the kind of heart that has blessed me as LaRosa's former pastor and the kind of heart that I know will bless you as you see it poured out on every page of this workbook.

Another thing that makes this workbook such a helpful resource is that LaRosa is a faithful practitioner of every method you are going to encounter. The Bible is not something to master for mere knowledge; rather, it is we who are to be mastered by the Bible. The Bible, by God's sovereign design, is to be transformative as well as informative; it is to govern our doctrine (what we believe) and devotion (how we are to live). The BibleStudy.Tips workbook will help you not merely acquire more knowledge or even correct knowledge, but show you how the tools and methods provided will help you, by God's Holy Spirit, be transformed and conformed by His Word.

With a world that is growing ever more hostile to the Bible (and the God of the Bible, by the way), with many churches growing ever more distant from the objective truth claims and caving in to cultural and secular pressure from all sides, and with many Christians having their ear tickled by every wind of doctrine, we need more everyday tools and resources like the BibleStudy.Tips workbook.

I am grateful for laypeople like LaRosa, gifted and empowered by the Holy Spirit to use their gifts and abilities in order to help not only laypeople, but pastors like me as well, become more faithful disciples of the Lord Jesus Christ. I know you will be blessed and encouraged.

Miles Rohde
Pastor, Redemption Spokane

How to Use This Workbook

Intimidated. Frustrated. Sheepish. Unmotivated. Disinterested. Wishful. Unsure. Baffled.

Do any of these words describe you when it's time to study your Bible?

Do you look at other Christians and wonder how they know so much about the Bible? Do you wonder how they see things you don't in the pages of Scripture? Are you at an impasse because your church or community expects you to already know how to study the Bible?

If we're honest, that's most of us; but, we're too embarrassed to admit it. This feeling leads many to shy away from ever engaging the Bible in any serious manner. Aside from Sunday mornings and an occasional devotional with a feel good Bible verse, our Bibles remained closed and unread.

That used to be me.

So let's be real with one another, Bible study is hard!

I won't try to convince you that Bible study is not hard. If I did, I would be lying to you.

But, you know what? Your frustration is a good thing! It means you care. If you didn't want to study God's Word, you wouldn't be bothered that Bible study is hard & you wouldn't be frustrated. Here's the important thing: if you're reading this book it means you are ready to do something about it, and that is a good thing.

I wrote this book to ease your frustration. While Bible study might be hard, learning how to study the Bible isn't as difficult as you might think. With the right tools you can unravel the enigma that is the Bible, understand it, and propel your faith.

What to Expect

Here's what you can expect from the BibleStudy.Tips workbook.

Over the course of 8 weeks, this workbook will walk you through a series of Bible study methods and techniques. These methods are the foundation you need to study God's

Word. Each method builds upon the previous one, so that by the end of 8 weeks you have the necessary skills and knowledge to feast daily on Scripture.

Making your way through this workbook will not be a cakewalk. At the same time, it won't be so difficult that you will want to give up. I do my best to explain each Bible study method as simple as possible with easy to follow steps. I then provide you with an example of what a completed study looks like, so you have a reference. After that, the rest of the week is up to you, as you work through the daily exercises of studying Scripture using each week's method.

As you work through this workbook, here are some guidelines to consider:

First, *trust the process*. Each Bible study method is tried & true. I am not teaching anything revolutionary, and these are methods of study Christians have used for years.

Second, *do not rush* through this workbook. While it is a relatively short read, the majority of your time will be spent working through the exercises and studying Scripture. To get the most out of this workbook, go through each week in order.

Next, *expect some setbacks*. You might find that after a week of using a particular method, you are not wholly comfortable with it. That's okay. Do not move to the next method until you are confident in your ability to use the current method. In the appendix, I have included additional material for each week, along with printable worksheets. Bible study is not a sprint, so take your time and learn to do it right.

Finally, *your success will be determined by the effort you put forth*. These Bible study methods do nothing on their own; they are only guides. It is only when you put them to work that you will reap the fruit of your efforts. So long as you are willing to put in the work that goes into learning and using each method, you will succeed.

Where Should I Use This Workbook?

There are many ways to use the BibleStudy.Tips workbook. It can be used for personal study or in a one-on-one discipleship setting. The workbook can also be used in a group setting, such as a classroom, Sunday school class, or church small group. The choice is yours. The book is able to adapt to most settings.

Personal Study

This workbook is ideal for personal Bible study. Everything you need to learn the Bible study methods is in this book. When using it on your own, you are free to move at your own pace, taking more time on each method as needed.

Discipleship or One on One

The BibleStudy.Tips workbook is also at home in a discipleship context. In such a scenario, it is recommended that the disciple maker be a week ahead in the material, so they can remain aware of the content that is ahead. Then work through the material with those they are discipling, teaching them the Bible study methods, answering any questions they have along the way.

Group Setting

If you are leading a group or class, the BibleStudy.Tips workbook also works well in this setting. Included with the book's bonus materials is a "Leader's Guide." This guide will help you facilitate discussion so the group gets the most out of the material. You can walk through the methods and then study a passage together as a group, or use a different method that best works for your context.

What Tools Do I Need?

Yes, you can grow in your faith with nothing more than a Bible. But, if you're going to mine the depths of God's Word, you need some additional tools. To get the most out of this workbook you need these tools at your disposal.

Every resource listed below can be obtained either as a physical book or digitally through various Bible software platforms. As you add them to your study library, I urge you to consider Bible software, as it comes with many benefits.[1] If financial resources are a limiting factor, know that you can find all of this information online at various Bible study websites, which are listed below.

---

[1] See the Appendix on how to build a Bible library (page 180). Also, go to page 205 to get great deals on Bible software.

Bible Study Tools

Here are the essential tools you need to get the most out of this workbook.

- The Bible (preferably one with cross-references)
- A good study Bible[2] (this can also serve as your Bible)
- Bible concordance
- Strong's dictionary
- Strong's exhaustive concordance
- Bible dictionary

Additionally, you may want to have the following, but know they are not necessary for completing the exercises in this workbook:

- Single volume Bible commentary
- Bible atlas
- Bible handbook

Bible Study Websites

The websites below will have the majority of what you need to complete any of the studies in this workbook.

- BlueLetterBible.org
- StudyLight.org
- BibleHub.com

Before you begin your 8-week journey, I will leave you with this one secret to success: cultivate a love for reading & curiosity. Both will go a long way to ensure a lifetime of hearing from God through his Word.

Grace & peace!

LaRosa Johnson

---

[2]See the Appendix on how to choose a good study Bible (page 184).

WEEK 1
Bible Journaling

*"I will meditate on your precepts and think about your ways.
I will delight in your statutes; I will not forget your word."
(Psalm 119:15-16, CSB)*

We live in an age where information flashes past us in the blink of an eye. One minute we're reading a Facebook post. The next moment we're reading a news story. Then it's over to YouTube to watch the latest trending video. Oh wait, now there's a Twitter thread coming in. Can't forget to check Instagram & Reddit.

The information never stops.

In a world where information moves so quickly, how do you slow your brain to intentionally remember something? Better yet, how do you set your time with God apart from the rest of your high speed life?

What if I told you there's a method that has been practiced for centuries that will not only help you with your Bible study, but will also help you remember what you've read. Would you be interested in this?

The method isn't anything new. You've probably heard of it, and possibly done it at some point in your life. It's called journaling, and it is a vital tool for Bible study success. If we are to know who God is and what he has done in our lives, we must journal.

Journaling lays the foundation you need to study and learn God's Word. So, we will begin with a simple journaling method that will help you take what you read in Scripture and put it to practice in your life.

Let's start with the necessary tools.

What You Need

To journal effectively, you don't need much. For this first Bible study method you only need the following:

- A Bible
- Notebook
- Pen or pencil

Why Journal?

You're probably asking yourself, "Why are we talking about journaling? I thought this book was about Bible study methods!" Yes, you are right. But, let me show you why journaling is important for Bible study.

First and foremost, journaling helps you remember. How do you remember the things that are worth remembering? If you're like me, you write them down. If you're going to remember someone's phone number or that list of things you need to get done, you put it somewhere you can look at it again, whether it be on a sticky note or in an app. Well, the same holds true for God's Word and how we study it. Whatever is not written down inevitably is forgotten.

Second, journaling teaches you to feed yourself from Scripture. So often we think we need others to break down the Bible for us, when we are quite capable of understanding God's Word for ourselves. Writing in a journal and recording your thoughts helps you digest what you've read by putting it into your own words.

Journaling also leaves a legacy. Journals are a timestamp of what happened in a given location at a set time in history. Over time, your journals become a written record of your time in the Word and what God has done in your life. This is something you can look back on in the future or during difficult seasons in life. And, it also serves as a testimony of your faith for those who come after you, such as your children and grandchildren.

Finally, journaling prevents Bible study from becoming an exercise where you simply check boxes. Far too often as Christians, we approach God's Word with the mindset that we need to get it done so we can move on to the next thing. We read our Bible reading plan & check the box with no memory of what we just read. Or, we read a quick devotional and call it good. Journaling slows us down and makes our time with God both intentional and thoughtful.

H.E.A.R.T. Journaling

So, now you're probably thinking to yourself, "Great, I don't have time as it is, and you want me to spend time writing long notes in a notebook?" Nope. Journaling doesn't have to be complicated or long, it only needs to be intentional. I will show you how simple journaling can be with a method called H.E.A.R.T. journaling.

H.E.A.R.T. stands for **Highlight**, **Explain**, **Apply**, **Respond**, and **Think**. Journaling the Bible in this way facilitates both understanding and application. As you go through the steps you will know what the Bible says and how God wants you to respond. Each step allows you to digest what you've read while letting God speak directly to your spirit. The H.E.A.R.T. method helps you hear from God through his Word.

This journaling method was originally developed by Robby Gallaty and the team at Replicate Ministries as H.E.A.R. journaling, a method I have used in my own Bible study. I have since expanded on their work by adding the "T," which adds biblical meditation[3] into the process of journaling.

Let's now look at the details of the H.E.A.R.T. journaling method.

Highlight

The first step in the process involves writing down four things at the top of your journal entry:

1. The date
2. The passage you read
3. A verse or two that stood out during your reading
4. A title for the passage that will help you remember it

That's all there is to highlighting the passage in your journal. You are making a note of what stood out in the day's reading.

Explain

The next step requires examination of the biblical text. Here you you want to answer questions like:

- Who wrote the passage?
- Who is the audience?
- Why was this book written?
- How does this passage fit with the rest of the book and the Bible as a whole?
- What is the passage saying?

---

[3] You can learn more about biblical meditation in the appendix (page 190)

The goal of this step is to help you understand the meaning of the text and how it would have been understood by its original hearers. This step moves you in the direction of making application from the text.

For more difficult passages, feel free to consult your study Bible or commentary to gain clarity. But, for now, I urge you to do as much as you can without consulting other resources.

Apply

Once you understand the meaning of the passage, the next step is to apply it to your life. This involves asking questions like:

- What does this passage mean today?
- What does this verse look like in my life?
- Is there anything in this passage God wants me to do or stop doing?
- How can it help me?

As you answer these questions you should be able to write down a few sentences about how God is speaking to you through the passage.

Respond

Next, you need to put action behind what you've read and the application you're to make. This can be either a clear action step you need to take after reading the passage, or it can be a prayer to God. No matter what the action is, you need to respond to the passage in some way.

Think

Finally, the last step involves thinking about the passage throughout the day as you have free moments. As you have moments in your day, meditate on the passage and its many facets. You can ponder things like:

- How does it impact your life?
- Have you fulfilled your action step for the day?
- What does this passage teach about God & Christ?
- How will this change how you relate to others?

- Why did that verse or two stand out?

If there is an immediate thought you want to think on throughout the day, write it in your journal. Otherwise, take a moment at the end of the day to reflect and write about how you meditated on the passage for that day.

Start Journaling Today

If you are going to improve your ability to study God's Word, you must keep a record of your growth. Bible journaling is your method for recording that growth. It might seem trivial at first, but your future self will thank you. Such a record of your faith will serve you well.

Turn the page and look at a couple examples of H.E.A.R.T. journals and then begin working through the exercises.

Highlight

Explain

Apply

Respond

Think

Example HEART Journal #1
December 28, 2017 — Acts 17 — Paul's Travels & Preaching

Highlight
Acts 17:3 - explaining and proving that it was necessary for the Christ to suffer and to rise from the dead, and saying, "This Jesus, whom I proclaim to you, is the Christ."

Explain
Paul is in three cities preaching the gospel and is chased out of the first two by unbelieving Jews. He moves on and keeps preaching the lordship of Christ and the salvation he offers. Paul doesn't let rough situations deter him from his work, but he keeps moving on.

Apply
I need to be more like the Bereans and diligent in my studies. Far too often I slack off when I know better. I also need to be willing to use what is around me to better share the gospel. Yet, this should never be a replacement for or diminish the gospel.

Respond
Heavenly Father, help me to be more faithful and diligent in my time with you.

Think
This verse is important because there are too many false teachings and teachers in the world. I must be like the Bereans who studied God's Word to make sure what they heard was true.

Example HEART Journal #2

December 29, 2017 — James 3:13-18 — Wisdom Contrasted

Highlight
James 3:17 - But the wisdom from above is first pure, then peaceable, gentle, open to reason, full of mercy and good fruits, impartial and sincere.

Explain
James is contrasting the wisdom of the world with what godly wisdom looks like. The world's wisdom is self-seeking. Godly wisdom is the opposite. It seeks to make peace and is motivated by outward works toward others, instead of being selfish.

Apply
Do my motives and behavior embody godly wisdom? I need to do a better job of daily listening to the Holy Spirit and live a life that embodies these traits. I know this is only done by the Holy Spirit's power and not my own strength.

Respond
Lord, I pray that you would help me today to live this truth, not just today but for the rest of my life. Help me live according to your wisdom.

Think
I thought about the fruit of the Spirit in Galatians 5 and how it compares to this passage. Living this way will have an immediate impact on my family and those around me.

Example HEART Journal #3

September 26, 2018 — Matthew 6:6 — Praying the Right Way

Highlight
Matthew 6:6 - But when you pray, go into your room and shut the door and pray to your Father who is in secret. And your Father who sees in secret will reward you.

Explain
Jesus is teaching his disciples to pray, but he doesn't want their time with the Father to be on public display because these are intimate and heartfelt conversations. It also shows the seriousness of prayer.

Apply
I cannot see God, but I know he hears my prayers, but I need to remember that I am actually talking to my Father and I can reveal my heart to him, and I know these times will be rewarding spiritually.

Respond
Father, help me to see my time with you as a priority.

Think
Intimate conversations happen behind closed doors. I don't pour out my heart to my wife in front of everyone, but I also make time to talk to her often. My relationship with God shouldn't be any different.

Workbook Exercises

Day 1
Genesis 12:1-20

Day 2
Ecclesiastes 12

Day 3
Daniel 6

Day 4
Romans 6

Day 5
2 Timothy 2

WEEK 2
Cross-Reference Study

"The people here were of more noble character than those in Thessalonica, since they received the word with eagerness and examined the Scriptures daily to see if these things were so." (Acts 17:11, CSB)

Do you want to study and use the Bible the way its authors did? What if you could examine and discuss Scripture the way Jesus did? That would be awesome, right? Well, it's possible; and, it's probably *the* best method of Bible study. If this was the only study method you learned, you'd be set for the rest of your Christian walk.

What is this Bible study method? It is the method of comparing Scripture with Scripture. This is what our Lord Jesus Christ did when he taught. Paul used this method frequently when making his arguments about the gospel. And we can use it too to understand Scripture.

How do we do this? Well, we're going to use those verse references that appear to the side of or beneath your Bible text. Those Bible verses are called cross-references. Their purpose is to hep you find passages related to the one you're currently studying.

If you let them, cross-references can be your best friend in Bible study, and they are at the heart of comparing Scripture with Scripture.

What You Need
The beauty of studying with cross-references is you don't need much. Like with journaling, all you need is:

- Your Bible
- Notebook
- Pen or pencil

Going forward, we will assume your Bible and notebook are necessary tools for study and no longer include them in the list.

Additionally, if you want to get fancy, you can add a cross-reference resource like the *New Treasury of Scripture Knowledge* or its predecessor (just drop "New" from the title).

What is a Cross-Reference?
At its simplest, a cross-reference is a marker in the text pointing to related content. When speaking of the Bible, cross-references point to verses containing related words and themes.

As you can see in the image below, cross-references are easy to spot in your Bible. The first number represents the Bible verse on the page being referenced. The text that follows the reference are Bible verses that contain similar content or themes as the verse it is referencing.

Cross-References in the ESV Study Bible

Now, not all cross-references are the same. You may notice different markings such as brackets, italicized text, or abbreviations before or after. These all have specific meanings and vary between Bibles & translations. For this reason, I recommend consulting your Bible's front matter to see how it uses cross-references and differentiates between the different types.

Why Use Cross-References?

Though there are many ways to study the Bible, it is best when we let the Bible and the context speak for itself. Some refer to this as using Scripture to interpret Scripture. Without having the Bible memorized, this is done through the use of cross-references.

Cross-references help you define and contextualize what you are reading. For example, when studying a difficult passage of Scripture, a cross-reference resource will point you to associated passages—many times relating to the topic or key word you are presently reading about, and sometimes a similar situation across the Biblical timeline. These related passages make it easier to figure out what is happening in the more difficult passage.

Cross-references should always be the first tool you consult when studying Scripture. When you let Scripture speak for itself it does a remarkable job. Joined together with the H.E.A.R.T. journaling method, this is the perfect way to understand a passage and dig deeper into God's Word.

How to Compare Scripture with Scripture

At first glance cross-references seem like a complicated system, but in practice their use is straightforward. There are only five steps you need to follow to compare Scripture with Scripture, and it mostly involves flipping pages and reading.

Step 1: Read the Passage

Focus only on the text at hand. Read and re-read the passage. Let the passage unravel itself without any outside help. As you study, write any observations you find in a notebook. The goal is to understand as much as you can about the passage on its own before consulting other tools.

Step 2: Look Up Cross-References

Once you've read your passage and have a general idea of what is being said, your next step is to turn to your cross-references. Look up each cross-reference one-by-one, reading its full context when necessary. Mark the cross-references that stand out or were helpful in explaining the original passage. As you mark your passages, make a quick note so you can remember why you marked it as helpful. Continue making notes as the cross-references unravel the meaning of the passage. All the passages you marked will be explored further in the next step.

Step 3: Look Up Your Cross-References' Cross-References

This is where the real fun begins. Because cross-references are all over the Bible, the verses you looked up will have their own cross-references. The next step is to look up their cross-references. Continue this process as time allows or until you're satisfied with how your cross-references have helped you understand your original passage or topic.

I recommend starting with the passages you marked as helpful in the previous step. Look up the cross-references for these passages first before moving on to the others. As you do this, you should see your original passaged listed in many of these cross-references. This will help you see the connection between passages and how the entire Bible fits together.

Step 4: Consult Other Study Tools

Once you've exhausted the cross-references in your Bible, turn to your other study tools if you still need help understanding the passage. Begin with another cross-reference tool like the *New Treasury of Scripture Knowledge*, which has far more extensive cross-references than your Bible.

From there, you can consult resources like the study notes in your Study Bible or a commentary. These tools can help you make sure you correctly interpreted the passage once you've completed your cross-reference work.

Step 5: Summarize the Passage

Finally, as you wrap up your study, you'll want to take all your work and summarize your findings. Write a note with your understanding of the passage, and then include the most relevant passages from your study so you can have them for future reference.

This is how I read my Bible most mornings. I sit at my desk with nothing more than my Bible and a notebook. I'll read the passage, follow the steps above, and complete my H.E.A.R.T. journal for the day.

The goal of this Bible study method is to use nothing more than your cross-references. It is intentionally simple, yet powerful. Even though Jesus and the Apostle Paul didn't have cross-references like we do, this is how they studied the Word of God: they compared Scripture with Scripture.

Let me repeat these words: Cross-references should always be the first tool you consult when studying Scripture. When you let Scripture speak for itself it does a remarkable job.

Bonus Tips

As we wrap up this Bible study method, here are a couple bonus tips for you.

First, the more you read the Bible, the more familiar it becomes. When this happens, sometimes you will read a passage and another will come to mind that's related. Most times, when you glance at your cross-references it'll be there. If it is, fantastic, your Bible knowledge is growing! But, sometimes it won't be listed. In these moments, **grab your pen and write it in the margin**. Just make sure the passage fits the context & the reference is correct before writing it down.

Finally, if you want to dig deeper, add a resource like the *New Treasury of Scripture Knowledge* to your library, like I mentioned above. It's an expansive collection of cross-references. This resource is like putting your Bible's cross-references on steroids. A Bible only has limited space for cross-references, but the *New Treasury of Scripture Knowledge* is about the same size as your Bible and only contains cross-references. Adding it to your library will blow the roof off your Bible study.

Ahead of the Game

When you learn to incorporate this method into your Bible study you will be ahead of the game. Most people never get this far in studying God's Word. So, let's continue to the exercises so you can master the art of comparing Scripture with Scripture.

1. **Read the Passage**

2. **Look Up Cross-References**

3. **Look Up the Cross-References' Cross-References**

4. **Consult Other Study Tools**

5. **Summarize the Passage**

Example Exercise
Ephesians 5:15-17

Summary
We only have a limited time on earth, so we need to be wise in how we live, particularly making the decision to live for God.

Cross-References
- v. 15 - Col. 4:5; Prov. 15:21
- v. 16 - Eph. 6:13; Eccl. 12:1; Amos 5:13; Gal. 1:4
- v. 17 - Rom. 12:2; 1 Th. 4:3; 5:18

Cross-Reference Summaries
- Col. 4:5 - walk in wisdom toward outsiders, make the best use of the time
  Xrefs - Mk. 4:11
- Prov. 15:21 - those with understanding walk straight
  Xrefs - Prov. 10:23
- Eph. 6:13 - put on the armor of God to stand in the evil day
  Xrefs - 1 Pet. 4:1
- Eccl. 12:1 - remember God in your youth
  Xrefs - Lam. 3:7; Eccl. 11:8; 2 Sam. 19:35
- Amos 5:13 - those who are evil should remain silent before a God who will judge them
  Xrefs - Eccl. 3:7; Mic. 2:3
- Gal. 1:4 - Jesus died for our sins to deliver us from this evil age
  Xrefs - Mt. 20:28; Rom. 4:25; 1 Cor 15:3; Eph 2:2; 1 Jn 5:19; Jn. 15:19; Phil. 4:20; 1 Th. 1:3; 3:11, 13

- Rom. 12:2 - renew your mind and be transformed, discerning God's will
  Xrefs - 1 Pet. 1:14; 1 Jn. 2:15; Tit. 3:5; Ps 51:10; 2 Cor 4:16; Eph 4:23; Col 3:10; Eph 5:10; 1 Th 4:3
- 1 Th 4:3 - our sanctification is God's will
  Xrefs - Rom 6:19, 22; 1 Cor 1:30; 2 Th 2:13; 1 Tim 2:15; Heb 12:14; 1 Pet 1:2; 1 Cor 6:18
- 1 Th 5:18 - give thanks in all circumstances
  Xrefs - Eph 5:20

New Combined Summary

We should seek to serve God from a young age and live in wisdom, knowing that Jesus has paid for our sins and desires for us to live godly lives that obey his will and avoid evil. We also learn God's will through studying his Word.

Workbook Exercises

Day 1
Colossians 3:1-4

Day 2
1 Timothy 2:1-4

Day 3
James 1:22-25

Day 4
1 John 1:5-7

Day 5
Matthew 22:37-40

WEEK 3
Bible Survey Study

"Appoint for yourselves three men from each tribe, and I will send them out. They are to go and survey the land, write a description of it for the purpose of their inheritance, and return to me." (Joshua 18:4, CSB)

One of the best ways to study the Bible is to do it one book at a time. You pick a book, and you go through it chapter-by-chapter and verse-by-verse until you reach the end of the book. But, so many Christians set themselves up for failure before they even begin. How, you ask? By failing to first get an overview.

When it comes to most things in life, we do not jump in without first knowing what we're getting ourselves into. We don't dive into a pool until we know how deep it is. The same goes for accepting a job, buying a home, getting married, and so on. We survey all the information before committing and diving in.

We should do the same with our Bible study. Before we begin an in-depth study of a book of the Bible, we should first get acquainted with it and know where we're about to spend our time. We can do this with a Bible study method called a Bible survey. This method is one of the best ways to get a general overview of a Bible book and its structure.

This week you will learn what a Bible survey is, why you should use them, and, most importantly, how to do it.

What You Need

Unlike the previous two weeks where you could complete a study with nothing more than a Bible, a Bible survey requires having some tools at your disposal. To complete this type of study you will need at least one of the following:

- Study Bible
- Bible Dictionary
- Bible Handbook

Additional Bible study tools you can use in this type of study are Bible surveys (such as an Old or New Testament survey) or commentaries.

If you do not have any of these resources, you can obtain the information you need using one of the many free websites listed in the "How to Use This Workbook" section at the beginning of this book (page xi).

What is a Bible Survey?

Before we get into the logistics of how to do this study, let's first explain what it is. At its simplest, a Bible survey is a study that provides a general overview of a book of the Bible. It is like flying in an airplane, the goal is to get a high-level look at a book of the Bible without getting overwhelmed by the details.

Bible surveys are meant to give you the 30,000 foot aerial view of what a book of the Bible is about. And, when done 66 times, you get the big picture of the Bible from Genesis to Revelation.

Why Bible Surveys?

The next logical question is, why do a Bible survey study? I mean, why not read the introduction in your study Bible and be satisfied? While that is certainly an option, that's like being handed the answers to a final exam. You will never take the time to learn the process if you're always given the answer. So, our goal is to show you how to get to the same conclusions that are found in your study Bible.

Here are a few reasons why Bible surveys matter:

- It prepares you for an in-depth study of a book of the Bible
- Bible surveys challenge you to think through the structure of a book and why it's organized that way
- Bible surveys help you know which books of the Bible to turn to when facing difficult life situations
- Having an overview of books of the Bible aides every area of Bible study

There are more ways a Bible survey can help your biblical knowledge and spiritual growth, but these are just a few.

How to Do a Bible Survey

Now we're ready for the fun part. Let's walk through the steps to complete a Bible survey.

As you will see, the steps are straightforward, but the process requires both work and research. With at least one of the above tools at your side, you are ready to begin.

The goal with a Bible survey is to walk away with your own abbreviated book introduction and outline, like you would find in your study Bible. Yes, some of the information will come from your study Bible, but you will still put in the work to study and process the information.

The process contains six steps:

1. Get the Background Information
2. Identify the Book's Theme and Subject
3. Find the Book's Divisions
4. Title Each Chapter
5. Outline the Book
6. Summarize the Book

So, let's begin.

Step 1: Get the Background Information

The first step is finding all of the background information so you can make sense of the book. The objective is answering questions like:

- Who wrote the book?
- When was the book written?
- To whom was the book written?
- Why was this book written?
- What was going on in world history that might have influenced this book?

Much of this information can be gleaned directly from your study Bible or Bible dictionary. In your study Bible, turn to the introduction for the book you're studying. For a Bible dictionary, find the book's entry. Some of the answers will be obvious. For example, we know Paul wrote the book of Romans to the church in Rome. We know this because Paul gives us this information in the opening verses of his letter. But, more important details, such as background information, are only found through the use of our study tools.

As you find the answers to these questions, jot down the details that are worth remembering in your notebook.

With your answers in hand, you will have a basic framework for understanding the book and its purpose, which means you're ready for the next step.

Step 2: Identify the Book's Theme and Subject

Next, identify the book's key theme(s) and subject(s). Again, the answers will be readily available in either your study Bible or Bible dictionary, which is fine to consult. But, I would challenge you to read through the book, especially if it's a shorter one, and identify these items yourself. Once you've done the work yourself, you can consult your study tools to compare notes.

It's important to note that while the authors of our study tools have lots of theological degrees and training, they take the same steps to get the answer. So, it's worth putting in the effort to do it on your own. All you're doing is making observations and writing them down in your notebook.

Step 3: Find the Book's Divisions

While the outlines in your commentary or study Bible are great, there's nothing like building your own outline from the ground up. The first step is looking for the book's major divisions and naming them. For example, as you read 1 Thessalonians two major divisions become evident:

1. Paul recounts his ministry with the Thessalonians (chs. 1-3)
2. Paul's teaching (chs. 4-5)

Within these major divisions, you can further divide it into subdivisions.

As you look for the major divisions, avoid referencing the outlines in your study resources. Don't take shortcuts just because they are there. Take your time and work through these so you can create your own unique outline.

When it comes to the subdivisions, the headings in your Bible are a great tool. That said, you don't have to follow those divisions, as your divisions can be more broad or granular. Also, compare multiple Bible translations, as they may utilize different divisions.

Step 4: Title Each Chapter

For the fourth step, give each chapter a unique title. List every chapter number on its own line in your notebook and write your titles beside each number. Look at each chapter and find its overall theme or subject, and use that as your title, putting it in your own words.

The purpose of this step is to help you internalize the book's information. As you come up with titles for each chapter you learn its content and theme, which helps you reference it in the future.[4] Also, as you do more in-depth studies in the future, this information helps you know what to expect when you reach each new chapter.

Step 5: Outline the Book

Fifth, write your outline. Look at the notes you took as you read through the book. Observe the natural breaks in thought and content. Take your work from steps 3 & 4 and synthesize it into your outline. The items from those steps will likely become the major points in your outline.

Create an outline with major divisions, and then each chapter, with subdivisions within each chapter.

With this step complete, consult the outlines in your study Bible or dictionary. Compare those outlines to your own. How similar is your outline to the ones in your study resources?

Step 6: Summarize the Book

Finally, summarize your findings. At this point, you know the following:

- Who wrote the book
- The recipients of the letter
- Why the book was written
- Background surrounding its writing
- The book's overall subject and theme

---

[4] I once knew a pastor who did this for every chapter in the Bible and had it memorized. As a result, he could easily tell you what any chapter was about. I always found that so amazing & wondered how he did it. This step is how.

- The book's structure (from your outline)

With this data in hand, in a sentence or two, write a succinct description of your book. Put this summary in your notebook. In addition, include any key verses that best summarize the book's message.

Once you've written your summary and key verses, your Bible survey study is complete. Now, you are equipped to begin a deeper study of that book, or move on to another book survey.

Summary

A Bible survey isn't difficult. All you need are the right tools, an eye for detail, and some patience. Now you're ready to begin working on Bible surveys of your own (and don't worry, we're not doing any big books).

1. Get Background Information

2. Identify the Theme & Subject

3. Find the Book's Divisions

4. Title Each Chapter

5. Outline the Book

6. Summarize the Book

Example Exercise
1 Thessalonians

Step 1: Background Information
Author & Recipients: the Apostle Paul to the church in Thessalonica. Silas and Timothy are listed as co-authors

Date: AD 49-51, likely during Paul's stay in Corinth

Purpose: the letter was written to address Paul's thoughts after his abrupt departure after 3 sabbaths, and answering questions that Timothy brought back, particularly questions about the timing of the Lord's return.

Step 2: Identify Theme & Subject
The major theme in this letter is Jesus' second coming. Each chapter addresses this issue and how Christians ought to respond.

Step 3: Find the Major Divisions
1. Paul recounting his ministry with the Thessalonians (chs. 1-3), and
2. Paul's teaching (chs. 4-5).

We can break down chapters 4 & 5 into several subdivisions:

1. Sanctification (4:1-12)
2. The Coming of the Lord (4:13-18)
3. The Day of the Lord (5:1-11), and
4. Final Exhortations (5:12-28)

Step 4: Title Each Chapter
1. Thanksgiving for a Good Example
2. Paul's Conduct and Example
3. Timothy's Encouraging Report
4. Sanctification and Christ's Return
5. Instructions on Holy Living

Step 5: Outline the Book
I. Ministry Reflections (1 Thess 1:1-3:13)
   A. Thanksgiving for a Good Example - Chapter One
      1. Greeting (1 Thess 1:1)
      2. Thanksgiving for a Good Example (1 Thess 1:2-10)
   B. Paul's Conduct & Example - Chapter Two
      1. Paul's Conduct & Example / Founding the Church (1 Thess 2:1-12)
      2. The Gospel: Received & Opposed (1 Thess 2:13-16)
      3. Longing to Visit the Church (1 Thess 2:17-20)
   C. Timothy's Encouraging Report - Chapter Three
      1. The Ministry of Timothy (1 Thess 3:1-5)
      2. Timothy's Encouraging Report (1 Thess 3:6-10)
      3. Prayer for the Church (1 Thess 3:11-13)
II. Instructional Teaching (1 Thess 4:1-5:28)
   A. Sanctification & Christ's Return - Chapter Four
      1. Sanctification and Purity (1 Thess 4:1-8)
      2. Disciplined Living (1 Thess 4:9-12)
      3. The Coming of the Lord (1 Thess 4:13-18)
   B. Instructions on Holy Living - Chapter Five
      1. The Day of the Lord (1 Thess 5:1-11)
      2. Instructions on Holy Living (1 Thess 5:12-22)
      3. Benediction (1 Thess 5:23-28)

Step 6: Summarize

1 Thessalonians is a book about a healthy church that Paul encourages to continue growing in holiness. The key verses are 1 Thessalonians 1:7-10 and 4:1.

Workbook Exercises

Day 1
Jonah

Day 2
Colossians

Day 3
Titus

Day 4
2 Peter

Day 5
Jude

WEEK 4
Topical Study

"if you seek it like silver and search for it like hidden treasure, then you will understand the fear of the LORD and discover the knowledge of God." (Proverbs 2:4-5, CSB)

The question inevitably comes up. You know the question. What does the Bible say about *that*? Depending on the topic, we may or may not have an answer. Sure, we know what the Bible teaches about salvation. But what does it teach about everyday matters like fear, anxiety, or patience? How do we find the answers to those questions? The best way to answer them is with a topical Bible study.

I want you to be able to answer those questions when they come your way, so that's why a topical Bible study is our fourth Bible study method. This week, not only will you learn all the steps you need to complete such a study, but you will learn a systematic way to know what the Bible teaches on any subject.

Let's start with the necessary tools for the job and why you would want to do a topical study.

What You Need

Along with your Bible and notebook, these are the tools you will need to complete this study:

- Bible concordance
- English thesaurus
- English dictionary
- Bible dictionary

Feel free to use online resources for the English dictionary and thesaurus. I often use dictionary.com or an app on my phone.

The following items are optional, but will enhance your topical study:

- Topical Bible (like *Nave's Topical Bible* or the *Thompson Chain Reference Bible*)
- Cross-Reference resource (like the *New Treasury of Scripture Knowledge*)

Why Do a Topical Study?

The main reason to do a topical study is so you can know what the Bible says about a given subject. But, that is not the only reason.

The objective of a topical study is to trace a theme or subject through the entirety of Scripture. Therefore, this type of study is applicable to all walks of life. Topical studies are great for parents wanting to know how to best raise their children. They are great for helping you know how to deal with various life issues. Topical studies can even prove fruitful when sharing the gospel.

The beauty of topical studies is they can be as simple or detailed as you want them to be. You can study complicated & involved subjects like the doctrine of the Holy Spirit. Or, you can study something more practical like how you should handle your money.

Topical studies are great because they help you learn your Bible in a way that makes application easy, while also teaching you to make use of some very simple, but essential, Bible study tools.

How to Do a Topical Study
Now that you know what a topical study is, let's dive into how to do it.

Step 1: Choose Your Topic
The first step in a topical study is choosing the topic. Don't overcomplicate this process. What interests you right now? What stood out in your daily Bible reading or survey study? Maybe you're reading 1 Thessalonians 4 and want to learn more about the topic of sanctification. Or, on a whim you become curious about what the Bible teaches on anger because it's something you're struggling with at the moment. There is no right or wrong way to decide on a topic, you just need to pick one.

For the remaining steps, let's assume you want to know what the Bible says about being "stressed out."

Pro Tip: A good habit to form as you study books of the Bible is to create lists of topics and subjects that are contained within each chapter. Not only will this help you better learn the information, but it gives you ideas for topical studies.

Step 2: Look for Related Words & Synonyms
Once you've chosen your topic, next, find any related words, phrases, or synonyms. Your goal in this step is to list anything that might be related to your word. Sticking with

the example topic of being stressed out, you would add related words like: anxiety, worry, fear, cares, and burden. If you need help finding additional words, use your thesaurus.

Also consider the inclusion of antonyms for your subject, especially if it is something negative. In terms of stress, you would want to also study topics like peace and contentment as possible solutions to stress.

At this point, you will probably have a long list of words and topics. That's okay. Instead of studying each one, pick a few key words to use as the foundation of your study.

Step 3: Define Your Word

Before you go further in your study, you need a firm grasp on the word(s) or topic(s) you're studying. This is why the next step is defining your words.

First, begin with an English dictionary. Look up your topic and make a note of its meaning. Next, turn to a Bible dictionary if it contains an entry for your topic, so you can also have a biblical definition.

Is there anything of interest in how the word is defined? If so, be sure to note that. This step can also prove to be a great place to find additional words to include in your study.

Step 4: Find Relevant Bible Verses

With your list of words in hand, find all the related Bible verses for your fourth step. There are a couple key tools you can use to find these verses.

The first tool at your disposal is a concordance, preferably an exhaustive concordance. To use the concordance, look up each word and any related words, like you would in a dictionary. You will then encounter a list of every Bible verse that has your word. This list is a good start, but it won't list verses on the topic where the word is not used explicitly. The next tool will solve this problem.

A topical Bible is the next tool you should consult. This tool takes the Bible's topics and themes and alphabetizes them into lists of relevant Bible passages. The advantage that a topical Bible has over a concordance is its listing of verses based on topic, even if the word is not explicitly used in the verse. Look up your words in the topical Bible and add any verses not in your concordance to your list.

The combination of a concordance and topical Bible will return a sufficient list of verses to read.

Additionally, cross-references are another tool you may want to utilize in your topical study. As noted in week 2, cross-references point you to other Bible verses, many of which are related topically. Many of the cross-references will already be listed in your concordance or topical Bible, but there may be more verses that get added to your list.

Step 5: Make Observations on Each Passage

Once you've compiled your list of verses, read each passage. As you read, make notes and observations about what the passage says about your topic. Are there warnings or promises that should be heeded? Does the biblical author command the reader to respond a certain way? Is your topic within a list of other topics?

Be sure to read the verse within its context. Observe what comes before and after the verse. Without understanding the proper context, you can easily derail your topical study and draw incorrect conclusions. Read with intent and understand the passage from the perspective of the original audience and how they would have understood it. Also, differentiate between passages that are descriptive (describing events) versus prescriptive (teaching).

This step is where you unravel what Scripture says, so be diligent. Your goal is to understand what the Bible says, and nothing more. And, if you have questions, write those down so you can find the answers later, whether it be in another passage or other resources.

Also, be aware that not every verse in your list will be relevant to your study. Yes, the word may be mentioned in a verse, but that does not mean it is applicable to understanding the topic. For instance, if you're studying the spiritual gift of tongues, you wouldn't need to include passages that reference "tongue" when talking about general speech or the body part (like in James 3). You only need to spend time on passages relevant to your topic.

Step 6: Organize the Data

After you've completed the task of reading the text and making notes, next you will organize your findings as the next step in your topical study. Look at your notes on each passage. Categorize your topic into subtopics as they revealed themselves in the text. Put all the verses together that speak positively of the topic, and do the same with the negative verses. As you go through this process, you will build a picture of what the Bible says on your topic. Sometimes it takes a little work to categorize the verses; but, more often than not, the categories will be obvious.

The outline you build at this step should provide a solid overview of what you've studied.

Step 7: Summarize & Apply

Once the data is organized, the only thing left to do is summarize your findings and make application.

With your outline in hand, you should be able to condense and summarize your findings into a couple sentences. At this step you should be able to say with confidence, "The Bible says ABC about topic XYZ."

From there, use your outline and summary to make application from the topic. You should be able to answer application questions like:

- How does this topic apply to the present day?
- How will my life change knowing what the Bible teaches on this topic?
- What is the application for the church?
- What will change in my prayer life after learning about this topic?
- How will this topic affect my family and those around me?
- Did my view on this topic change after this study?
- How does this topic help me understand God better?

That's all there is to a topical study.

What Can I Do with My Topical Study?

So, you may be asking yourself, "What can I do with a topical study once I've completed it?" That's a good question and one worth asking.

The first thing you should do with anything you study in Scripture is internalize and apply it to yourself. Without personal application, your studies are fruitless. You study first and foremost for yourself and your desire to grow closer to the Lord. Anything that comes as an extension of that is a bonus.

That said, the next thing you can do with your topical study is use it as an outline to teach others. Let's say you completed a topical study on anxiety and stress, you now have in your hands an outline of what the Bible says on the topic. You can use your subtopics as the foundation for a teaching outline. This is perfect for leading a Sunday school class, small group, or even family devotions.

Lastly, you can use the fruit of your topical study as a tool for future encouragement. For example, if your struggle with patience led you to do a topical study on the subject, you now have a list of verses to reference when you find yourself becoming impatient.

Let's Get to Work!

Now that you know the in's & out's of how to do a topical study, there's nothing left but to do it. Turn the page and begin working your way through some topical studies.

1. Choose a Topic

2. Find Related Words & Synonyms

3. Define the Word

4. Find the Relevant Bible Passages

5. Make Observations

6. Organize the Data

7. Summarize & Apply

Example Exercise
Thirst

Step 1: Choose a Topic
I've been reading the Beatitudes in Matthew 5 and am curious about the topic of thirst after reading Matthew 5:6 which says, "Blessed are those who hunger and thirst for righteousness, for they will be filled" (CSB).

Step 2: Find Related Words & Synonyms
Related words include: thirsty, yearning, hunger, hungry, parched, longing

Step 3: Define the Word
Thirst is a feeling of needing or wanting to drink something

Steps 4 & 5: Find Relevant Bible Passages & Make Observations
Bold text signifies key passages

- Exod 17:3 - thirst in the wilderness - physical
- Deut 8:15 - thirst in the wilderness, referring to a dry land - physical/land
- Deut 28:48 - physical thirst as punishment for disobedience - physical
- Judg 4:19 - physical thirst - physical
- Judg 15:18 - physical thirst - physical
- Ruth 2:9 - need for drink filled - physical
- 2 Sam 17:29 - need for drink filled - physical
- 2 Sam 23:15 - need for drink - physical
- 1 Chron 11:17 - same as previous verse (word for word)
- 2 Chron 32:11 - thirst used as threat to divert people from following Hezekiah - physical

- Neh 9:15, 20 - God provided supernaturally for Israel's thirst - physical/supernatural
- Job 5:5 - fools come to ruin & desire the things of others - material
- Job 22:7 - physical need for drink withheld - physical
- Job 24:11 - people work near the things they need but cannot partake - physical/material
- **Ps 42:2** - desire for God - spiritual
- **Ps 63:1** - desire for God - spiritual
- Ps 69:21 - food & drink used for mocking - physical
- Ps 104:11 - need for drink filled - physical
- Ps 107:5 - desire for food & drink in wilderness - physical
- Ps 107:9 - God fulfilled need for drink & food - physical/supernatural
- Ps 107:33 - God can cause draught - physical/land
- Prov 25:21 - meet the physical needs of your enemy - physical
- Isa 5:13 - thirst as punishment for disobedience - physical
- Isa 21:14 - physical need for thirst met - physical
- Isa 29:8 - longing for water/drink - physical
- Isa 32:6 - the fool does not provide for the needs of the hungry & thirsty - physical
- Isa 35:7 - the dry land will receive water - physical/land
- Isa 41:17 - God will not abandon the weak & needy who hunger & thirst - physical/supernatural
- Isa 44:3 - water will be given to dry land as a blessing, like he will give his Spirit - physical/land
- Isa 48:21 - water given in the wilderness - physical/supernatural
- Isa 49:10 - God will guide the thirsty to water - physical/supernatural
- Isa 50:2 - God can cause drought - physical/land
- Isa 55:1 - God will provide for his people - physical/supernatural/spiritual
- Isa 65:13 - God will withhold water from wicked people - physical/supernatural
- Jer 2:25 - physical thirst - physical
- Jer 31:25 - God satisfies thirst - physical/supernatural/spiritual

- Lam 4:4 - Infants need food/drink - physical
- Ezek 19:13 - metaphor for Israel in captivity & the type of land they're in - parable
- Hos 2:3 - metaphor for Israel & how God will punish them - parable
- Amos 8:11 - context of sending a famine of the word, not for food or water - supernatural/spiritual
- Amos 8:13 - physical thirst punishment for disobedience - physical
- **Matt 5:6** - thirst for God & righteousness - spiritual
- Matt 25:35 - meeting needs of others - physical
- Matt 25:37, 42, 44 - meeting needs of others - physical/spiritual
- John 4:13-15 - physical water temporarily satisfies, metaphor for eternal life - physical/spiritual
- John 6:35 - metaphor for eternal life - spiritual
- **John 7:37** - metaphor for eternal life - spiritual
- John 19:28 - need for refreshment - physical
- Rom 12:20 - meet the needs of your enemy - physical
- 1 Cor 4:11 - description of Paul's circumstances - physical
- 2 Cor 11:27 - description of Paul's circumstances - physical
- **Rev 7:16** - relief in heaven for those rescued from tribulation - physical/spiritual
- **Rev 21:6** - metaphor for eternal life - spiritual
- **Rev 22:17** - metaphor for eternal life - spiritual

Step 6: Organize the Data

Physical Thirst
- God fills the need for physical thirst - Neh. 9:15, 20; Ps. 104:11; 107:5, 9; Isa 41:17; 44:3; 48:21; 49:10; 55:1; Rev. 7:16
- God uses thirst as punishment for disobedience - Deut. 28:48; Isa. 5:13; 50:2; 65:13; Ezek. 19:13; Hos. 2:3; Amos 8:11, 13

Spiritual Thirst
- A desire or longing for God - Psalm 42:2; 63:1
- Description of eternal life - Isaiah 55:1; Jeremiah 31:25; John 4:13-15; 6:35; 7:37; Rev. 21:6; 22:17

Step 7: Summarize & Apply

Thirst is a physical human need for survival, but it also describes the spiritual condition we have toward God. As spiritual beings we should thirst for God, who is the only one who can satisfy and provide living water (eternal life).

We also need to be aware that God is the one who controls the heavens, including our supply of water. He can allow rain to fall or withhold it. We should be thankful for the water he supplies, both physical and spiritual. And what we do have, we should be generous to share with others, including our enemies, as this is a sign of our character as believers.

Workbook Exercises

Day 1
Baptism

Day 2
Reconciliation

Day 3
Freedom

Day 4
Passover

Day 5
Abiding

WEEK 5
Character Study

"But the LORD said to Samuel, "Do not look at his appearance or his stature because I have rejected him. Humans do not see what the LORD sees, for humans see what is visible, but the LORD sees the heart."" (1 Samuel 16:7, CSB)

We all have our favorite Bible characters and stories. Growing up, I always enjoyed the story of Samson's strength. As an adult, I've come to love James, the half-brother of Jesus Christ. Who are some of your favorite people or stories in the Bible? Why are they your favorites?

Because those people are your favorite, I'm sure you've read about them multiple times. But, have you ever slowed down and examined their lives in detail? There is so much we can learn about God, his people, and ourselves if we take the time to dig deeper. We can do this with a Bible study method called a character study.

With a character study you can learn things integral to the larger picture of Scripture, the kind of things that only come from intently examining the life of those the Bible writes about. Not only will you learn about your favorite Bible characters, but you will deepen your knowledge of God's Word.

What You Need

The necessary tools for a Bible character study are minimal, but helpful. Here's what you will need:

- Bible Dictionary
- Study Bible
- Topical Bible
- Bible Handbook (optional)

What is a Character Study?

In its most general sense, a character study is an analysis of the traits and qualities of a person or literary character. The goal is to understand as much as you can about the person being studied.

Authors often conduct character studies of their own characters before they begin writing a book or story. This work gives them the necessary knowledge to expertly craft their story, knowing how each character will react to the story's various developments.

Readers do similar work as they read these stories. But, instead of doing the work upfront like an author, the reader's work is on the backend as they analyze each character's development throughout the story.

When it comes to Bible study, a Bible character study is no different. It involves the same work as the reader of any story. The only difference is these are the accounts of real people and your goal is to see how they fit in the larger meta narrative of Scripture. As you learn about these people you learn about God, the gospel, and how you ought to conduct yourself as a believer.

Why do a Bible Character Study?

In the New Testament, Paul told the Corinthian church that what happened in the Old Testament was not mere happenstance. Instead, everything that happened was written down to serve as an example for its readers to learn from (1 Corinthians 10:11). This is why Bible character studies are important. They help you enter the lives of those who are written about in the Bible so you can learn how you ought to live in relation to God.

No matter the amount of information you have about a Bible character, there is something you can learn from their life. Every person is important and in the Bible for a reason. It's your job to find out why.

How to do a Bible Character Study

On the surface, a Bible character study might seem quite involved, but the process is simple once you get into it. Let's look at each step in detail.

Step 1: Choose a Bible Character

The first step is the most fun, simply pick a Bible character you want to study. This can come in the middle of a deeper study, or it can be done as a standalone study. The choice is yours. Don't overcomplicate this step. Pick a person and run with it.

Step 2: Find the Relevant Passages

Once you've chosen your person, find all the relevant Bible passages for that person.

Depending on the person you're studying, this process can be more challenging than at other times. For example, you would find information about Sarah mostly in Genesis, but she is also mentioned in places like Galatians. Yet, David's name is all over the Bible, so you would need to be more selective in what you include.

There are a few tools you can use to find out where your Bible character is mentioned. These tools include: 1) a concordance, 2) a Bible dictionary, and 3) a Bible handbook. You might even find help in a topical Bible. Look up your person's name and make a list of all the passages you need to study.

Step 3: Study the Bible Character

The third step is an all-inclusive study of your person and learning everything you can about them. This step involves a combination of reading all the Bible passages and any additional Bible study tools you have, like Bible dictionaries or your study Bible.

You can break this step down further by using the six basic questions you were taught in school: who, what, where, when, why, and how.

Step 3a: Who?

The first question you need to ask is "who is this person?" Here you want to ask a series of questions like:

- What does their name mean?
- Who are their parents?
- What's their lineage?

Step 3b: When?

The next question is "when." Seek to find answers to questions like:

- When did they live?
- What other events were going on in the Bible?
- What else was happening in world history during this period?

Answering these questions will give you a better picture of the events that shaped this person's life.

Step 3c: Where?

Location, location, location. After who and when, where is the next question up to bat.

- Where did this Bible character live?
- What impact did this have on their life?
- Is there anything notable or important about this location?

Just like the timeframe is important, location is just as important. Is the action happening in Egypt, the Promised Land, or Rome? This information plays a pivotal role in understanding the character you're studying and how their circumstances affected them.

Along with reading Scripture, this is a time when Bible maps can be a helpful aide to your studies, so make liberal use of them alongside your other Bible study tools.

Step 3d: What & Why?

Who, what, and where are the preliminary questions you need to ask. These are the questions that give you basic background about the person you're studying. When it comes to learning about the characteristics and qualities of your person, you need to start asking other questions. The first question you should ask is "what" and then "why," which includes questions such as:

- What do you learn about this person?
- What's their character? The good, bad, etc?
- Are they a good or bad example?
- How did this person affect others?
- Why did they act the way they did?

You will get the answers to these questions by reading the passages that reference your Bible character. It's here that you find out all you need to know about the person's character and how they interact with those around them.

If you find this part of your study moving slow, that's okay. Answering this question is where you will spend the majority of your time because it requires the most reading, note taking, and thought. It also requires wrestling with the text as you learn everything you can about your Bible character. Don't rush this question, otherwise you will miss out on the benefits that come with grinding it out. That being said, don't be afraid to lean on your Bible commentaries to help you out when you get stuck or when it comes time to double check your findings.

Step 3e: How?
With all the "W" questions out of the way, the only question left to answer is "how?" The focus of this question is looking at the biblical text and seeing how this person's life illustrates biblical principles. It is also focused on how God moved (or didn't move) in their life.

- How did God move or interact with this person during their life?
- What biblical principles can we glean from their life?
- How is the gospel displayed in this person's life?
- What does this person's life teach you about your relationship with God?

This question goes beyond the superficial and makes sure you're not forgetting the Bible's most important character: God. If you fail to see how God is moving and working in someone's life, then you are missing a key aspect of your Bible character study. Whether it is obvious in the text or you glean it from principles, you should be able to see how God worked. Even with a book like Esther where God's name is never mentioned you can still see him working.

Step 4: Organize & Summarize the Material
Once you've finished reading about your Bible character and answered all the questions, you must organize your findings. Your notes won't make much sense when you look back on it in the future if it remains a jumbled mess. This is why you should take time to rearrange your notes into something intelligible that you can later use as a reference tool. Here are some ideas for things you might want to have in your notes:

- A chronology or timeline of the character's life & ministry
- The major events in that person's life
- Key Bible passages that summarize or highlight their life
- Principles you learned based on their life
- Why they are important in the biblical narrative

With everything you've studied, you should be able to write a brief character sketch summarizing your Bible character study, which you can then file away for future studies.

Step 5: Find the Application

After organizing & systematizing all the data, the final step is figuring out how to apply this information to your life. So, wrap up your study by answering the following questions:

- How will you live differently after learning about this character's life?
- How should you respond to this person's example?
- Are there things you should start or stop doing after learning about this person?
- What does this person's life teach you about your relationship with God?
- How can you better worship God after learning about this person?
- How does this character affect how you share and live out the gospel?

The goal of all Bible study is twofold: 1) learning about God, and 2) applying what you've read so you can grow to look more like Christ. So, make sure your Bible character study ends with application of the biblical text. If what you've learned does not affect your life in some way then you have missed the point. Even if the application is simple, you should find at least one thing you can take away from a Bible character's life, no matter how much or little is written about them.

Let's Get to Work!

Now that you know how to do a Bible character study, you're ready to do your own. Turn the page and begin working your way through this week's exercises.

1. **Choose a Bible Character**

2. **Find the Relevant Passages**

3. **Study the Person (Who, What, Where, When, Why & How)**

4. **Organize & Summarize**

5. **Find Application**

Example Exercise
Jude

Step 2: Relevant Passages
Matthew 12:46, 47; 13:55; Mark 3:31, 32; 6:3; Luke 8:19, 20; John 2:12; John 7:1-10; Acts 1:14, 15; 1 Corinthians 9:5; Jude 1

Step 3: Study the Person

Who?
- Jude: another form of Judas, which is the Greek transliteration of the Hebrew name Judah, which means "Praise Yahweh."
- Parents: Joseph & Mary
- Siblings: Jesus Christ (half brother), James, Simon, Joseph, other brothers & sisters

When?
Jude lived in the First Century and is a contemporary of Jesus Christ. There are no exact dates when he was born, but was definitely a younger brother of Jesus.

At this time, the nation of Israel is under Roman rule, and the religious leaders are the Pharisees & Sadducees.

Where?
It is likely that Jude grew up in Nazareth in Galilee, like Jesus. He also potentially travelled with Jesus during his earthly ministry.

We know that he was in Jerusalem in the Upper Room after the death of Jesus (Acts 1:14-15), waiting for the Holy Spirit's arrival. After this we do not know of his whereabouts.

What & Why?
At the beginning of Jesus' ministry, his brothers were skeptical of him being the Messiah, and could probably be labeled as unbelievers (John 7:5). They likely had political aspirations for Jesus if he was the Messiah, and wanted him to perform miracles in the open. It is easy to see why this would be so, having grown up with Jesus and knowing him personally.

At some point after Jesus' death and resurrection, Jude (and his brothers) believe in Jesus as the Messiah. This created a radical change in thought and behavior, moving from skeptic to church leader. This is a great example of how the gospel can radically transform lives.

Jude's leadership within the church led him to write a letter warning against false teaching in the church (book of Jude).

How?
The way God worked in the life of Jude is similar to that of those who grow up in the church. He grew up learning the ways of God (Judaism) and even witnessed the mighty works of God in Jesus. Yet, it wasn't until the gospel became personal that he believed, when he witnessed the resurrected Christ. Yet, when he believed, his life was never the same.

This goes to show that we cannot always expect the work of God in someone's life to be immediate. Sometimes it takes a lifetime, and that's okay. God will move us on his own timeline. But, when we are changed, it should transform who we are.

Step 4: Organize & Summarize

Jude/Judas/Judah
Half-Brother of Jesus Christ, Church leader

Major Events: Unbeliever/Skeptic to Believer & Leader

Key Verse: Jude 3-4

Principles: God moves on his own timeline

Step 5: Find Application
God can and will save whomever he will whenever he chooses; but, when he does, our lives should never be the same. Like Jude, I need to go from someone who did not believe to someone who earnestly contends for the faith.

Workbook Exercises

Day 1
Gideon

Day 2
Rahab

Day 3
James (the brother of Jesus)

Day 4
Joseph (husband of Mary)

Day 5
The Samaritan Woman

WEEK 6
Word Study

"""Law after law, law after law, line after line, line after line, a little here, a little there."" (Isaiah 28:10, CSB)

When people talk about studying the Bible, one thing they always want to learn to do is a word study. I have to admit, of all the ways you can study God's Word, it's one of the most interesting and fun. There is a level of mystery and fascination that comes from working with ancient foreign languages and seeing how it moves into modern language.

Yet, for as fun as word studies can be, there are more important ways to study God's Word, which is why it is only now being introduced. When it comes to learning God's Word, the previous methods go much further in developing your understanding of the Bible. But, now that you have those concepts down, it's time to learn how to do word studies.

So, prepare for some fun digging into the Bible's original languages.

What You Need

A word study requires tools you have yet to use in your studies. These are specialized tools, but are not difficult to use. For ease of use, I recommend using them in a Bible app or using one of the online resources mentioned in the "How to Use This Workbook" section at the beginning of this workbook. Here's what you're going to need to get a word study done:

- Bible with Strong's Numbers
- Strong's Dictionary or Lexicon
- Exhaustive Strong's Concordance
- Englishman's Concordance (optional)

Why Do a Word Study?

Since the Bible is already available in our language, what is the point of word studies? Well, here are two very important reasons.

First, the meaning of words change with time. Most people only understand a word's meaning in its current context. But, what did that word mean 100 years ago? For example, you can no longer assume the word "bad" means something of poor quality; nowadays it can mean "good" depending on its context. Consider the King James Version of the Bible. An English word you're reading in the KJV might mean something completely different to the original translators than it does in modern English (visit

KJVquiz.com to see what I mean). So, when it comes to Bible study, you must make it your goal to understand what the word meant to the biblical author.

Second, translating the Bible is a difficult job and there's not always a clear translatable equivalent. An example of this is the German word *blitzkrieg*, which has no real English equivalent. Instead, we use the German word without finding a comparable English word. This is one reason why there are so many modern Bible translations. Language remains in flux, so translators wrestle with the best way to communicate what the biblical authors wrote in modern language. So, if you want to best understand what a word means, you should turn to the original languages and do a word study.

The ultimate goal behind Bible word studies is to get a grasp on biblical concepts you would not get by reading the Bible alone. Digging into the words behind your English Bible can provide the knowledge needed to build better biblical understanding.

What's the Difference Between a Topical Study & a Word Study?

Before we move forward, there is a question you're probably wondering: what's the difference between a topical study and a word study? As you will soon see, the two appear quite similar. In terms of the process, they are nearly identical. But, there are some key distinctions between the two types of study.

A topical study is concerned with ideas and themes as they appear in Scripture. Your objective is answering the question, "What does the Bible say about this topic?" This means you often read passages that imply your topic, but do not directly reference it.

On the other hand, the job of a word study is to look up every occurrence of a word in the Bible to learn about its usage and meaning. This involves the use of specialized tools to get to the underlying Hebrew, Aramaic, or Greek our English words are translated from. Here the focus is on individual words and their meaning, and less on larger concepts and ideas. With a word study, the goal is to synthesize an author or the Bible's use of a given word.

The key difference is this: a word study works with specific words, but a topical study looks at themes and ideas in Scripture.

How to Do a Word Study

With the logistics out of the way, let's get into the nitty gritty of how to do a word study. As already stated, the steps will look similar to a topical study, but will take some clear divergences.

Step 1: Find a Word to Study

The first step is finding the right word to study. Generally speaking, word studies are born out of other studies, such as working your way through a book of the Bible. Thus, the right word is dictated by your study. As you read through a passage of Scripture, a word or two will catch your eye & pique your curiosity. When that happens, you've found a word worth studying.

Step 2: Find the Strong's Number

Once you've found a word to study, you need to find the underlying Greek or Hebrew word so you can dig deeper. This is done with a system called Strong's Numbers, developed by the Methodist Bible scholar James Strong.

Without going into great detail, the Strong's numbering system gives a number to every Greek and Hebrew word in the Bible. These words are alphabetized and given a number, with Greek words prefixed with a "G" and Hebrew words an "H." So, when Bible translators translate the Bible, they are translating from one of these languages. There are some Bibles (Strong's and Interlinear Bibles) that align these translated words with their Greek or Hebrew equivalents. This makes it easy for those unfamiliar with the original languages to still study the Greek & Hebrew on some level.

The Strong's numbering system is similar to a dictionary, where you use the Strong's number to look up each word. In a Strong's Bible you will find the word you want to study, and note its Strong's number.

In a Bible app, Strong's numbers are easy to find. Refer to your software's tutorials for specific instructions on how to do this. But, if you're doing it by hand, you will either use an Interlinear Bible and note the Strong's number, or you will use your Strong's concordance to look up the word you want to study and then find the passage you're studying to see it's Strong's number.

As an aside, the NIV translation uses a number system similar to Strong's called GK numbers, which is basically an expanded & updated Strong's. Both work exactly the same.

With the Strong's number in hand, you can move to the next step.

Step 3: Consult a Strong's Dictionary or Lexicon

Next you need to look up your word in a dictionary or lexicon. In your Strong's dictionary or lexicon, find the entry for your Strong's number.

The Strong's dictionary will provide you with preliminary information about the word in question. You can expect to find its meaning, some basic glosses (English translations), as well as the number of times the word appears in the Bible. While not elaborate, this information primes the pump before moving to the next step.

Step 4: Find All Occurrences

For the fourth step, find all the occurrences of your word in the Bible. To find this information you will need to turn to your Strong's concordance. Like you did in the dictionary, find the entry for your Strong's number. Here you will find a list of every verse where your word appears in the Bible. If you use Bible software, this step can be done with a quick search of the Strong's number in the Bible (again, refer to your software's tutorials to learn how to do this).

With a list of every occurrence, your task is to now read every verse where that word is found. As you read, make notes about the word's usage and how it might be translated. Make note of the author of your original passage. How do they use the word in other writings?

Step 5: Summarize Your Study

At this point, you've done the hard work of uncovering the lexical range of your word. All that's left is to summarize your notes and how the Bible uses that Greek or Hebrew word. In a sentence or two, summarize the word's usage & meaning, particularly how it relates to the passage you're studying.

If you've done a topical study, this is information you can include or append to that study.

Go Deeper

This Bible study method focuses on a simple word study, but you can expand your study further. Learn the steps to do an advanced word study by viewing the in-depth guide on our website: https://biblestudy.tips/how-word-study.

It's Your Turn

Now you know the in's & out's of doing a Bible wordy study. It might seem complicated, but it's an easy & straightforward process once you get the hang of it. I'm sure once you get started doing word studies, you'll have a hard time stopping.

If you're ready to begin your own word studies, turn the page and get started!

1. Find a Word to Study

2. Find the Strong's Number

3. Consult a Strong's Dictionary

4. Find & Lookup All Occurrences

5. Summarize Your Study

Example Exercise

1 Thessalonians 2:1-8

1 For you yourselves know, brothers and sisters, that our visit with you was not without result. 2 On the contrary, after we had previously suffered and were treated outrageously in Philippi, as you know, we were emboldened by our God to speak the gospel of God to you in spite of great opposition. 3 For our exhortation didn't come from error or impurity or an intent to deceive. 4 Instead, just as we have been approved by God to be entrusted with the gospel, so we speak, not to please people, but rather God, who examines our hearts. 5 For we never used flattering speech, as you know, or had greedy motives--God is our witness--6 and we didn't seek glory from people, either from you or from others. 7 Although we could have been a burden as Christ's apostles, instead we were gentle among you, as a nurse nurtures her own children. 8 We cared so much for you that we were pleased to share with you not only the gospel of God but also our own lives, because you had become dear to us. (CSB)

Step 1: Find a Word to Study
The word "approved" in verse 4

Step 2: Find the Strong's Number
Approved is Strong's number G1381

Step 3: Consult a Strong's Dictionary
Greek word: dokimazō

22 occurrences in the New Testament

Definition: 1 to test, examine, prove, scrutinize (to see whether a thing is genuine or not), as metals. 2 to recognize as genuine after examination, to approve, deem worthy (Enhanced Strong's Lexicon).

Step 4: Find & Lookup All Occurrences
- Luke 12:56 - "interpret" (2x) - examining nature versus biblical times
- Luke 14:19 - "try out" - examining & testing out animals
- Romans 1:28 - "think" - failure to acknowledge God
- Romans 2:18 - "approve" - agreement based on examination
- Romans 12:2 - "discern" - knowing what God's will is & it's characteristics
- Romans 14:22 - "approves" - approval of conscience
- 1 Corinthians 3:13 - "test" - testing of works on day of judgment
- 1 Corinthians 11:28 - "examine" - self examination for communion
- 1 Corinthians 16:3 - "recommend" - recommend based on prior examination or approval
- 2 Corinthians 8:8 - "testing" - testing character/motives
- 2 Corinthians 8:22 - "tested" - tested through examination/work
- 2 Corinthians 13:5 - "examine" - we must test ourselves to see if we are in the faith
- Galatians 6:4 - "examine" - self examination
- Ephesians 5:10 - "testing" - test what we do according to God's standards
- Philippians 1:10 - "approve" - agreement based on examination
- 1 Thessalonians 2:4 - "approved" & "examines" - God approves & examines
- 1 Thessalonians 5:21 - "test" - we should test all things
- 1 Timothy 3:10 - "tested" - examination of potential deacons
- 1 Peter 1:7 - "is refined" - proving & examining of character
- 1 John 4:1 - "test" - testing things to see if they are from God or another source

Step 5: Summarize Your Study
The word dokimazō has to do with the idea of examining or testing something, which aligns with our definition in step 2. This word is mostly found in Paul's writings and refers to examining one's self. In the case of 1 Thessalonians 2:4, God is the one approving or examining Paul and his co-laborers for the work of ministry. Additionally,

dokimazō is used twice in this verse. This isn't obvious in the CSB because the second time it is translated as "examines."

As it relates to our verse (1 Thessalonians 2:4), not only does God test people, like on the day of judgment (1 Cor. 3:13), but he is currently testing our hearts—specifically as it relates to our usefulness for ministry.

Workbook Exercises

Day 1
Read Psalm 1. Find a word to study from the passage

Day 2
Ecclesiastes 8

Day 3
Luke 11:1-13

Day 4
1 Peter 4:12-19

Day 5
2 John

WEEKS 7&8
Inductive Bible Study

"Now God has revealed these things to us by the Spirit, since the Spirit searches everything, even the depths of God." (1 Corinthians 2:10, CSB)

Have you ever sat in church on a Sunday and wondered how your pastor pulled all those points out of the passage? It almost seems magical how he's able to articulate point after point from a handful of verses. Then you think to yourself, "I'll never be able to do that." Well, I want to let you know that you're well on your way to being able to do the same thing.

Everything you've learned in the last six weeks has built a foundation for richer and deeper Bible study. Every skill has built upon the previous one, and it all culminates in these last two weeks of study. Over the course of these final two weeks you will learn a method called inductive Bible study. It is one of the best ways to study God's Word and it utilizes all the skills you've learned up to this point.

We'll be using Richard Alan Fuhr Jr. & Andreas J. Köstenberger's fantastic book titled *Inductive Bible Study* as the general outline for this method. So, if you're ready, let's dive in!

What You Need

The inductive Bible study method is our most involved method, and thus will use every Bible study tool you have at your disposal.

What is Inductive Bible Study?

At its simplest, inductive Bible study is a straightforward step-by-step approach to interpreting and studying the Bible. It is time tested and generally regarded to be the best way to study Scripture.

Unlike deductive study, which begins with hypotheses and assumptions, inductive study begins with and only uses the evidence at hand. Conclusions are drawn from the facts presented by the evidence. This is how you want to interpret the Bible. You understand Scripture based on what it says, not your preconceived notions of what you want or assume the text says.

The inductive Bible study method helps you understand Scripture and make application for your life. It treats the Bible with respect, as the Word of God, and slows you down so you don't move haphazardly.

How Should You View the Bible?

Interpreting the Bible right requires viewing it through the proper lens. The Bible is: old, a compilation of many writings, and a religious book. You must keep all these things in mind when you study it. In addition, each facet plays a role in your interpretation.

First, the Bible is a historical book. It is several thousand years old and was written over centuries. This means you cannot approach it like a book written in the 21st Century. You must keep in mind the differences in culture and background when studying. Not to mention, the Bible's authors wrote in Hebrew, Aramaic, and Koine (common) Greek. These languages are old and require translation into modern vernacular.

Second, the Bible contains several literary genres. You cannot read each book of the Bible the same way. Scripture contains history, prophecy, letters, apocalyptic literature, poetry, and so on. Each passage should be understood based on its genre.

Finally, the Bible is a theological book. God wrote and teaches us about himself in the Bible. This truth must be at the forefront of your interpretation.

This triad shapes how you will move through the inductive Bible study method. Now, let's move into the how to of inductive Bible study.

How to Do Inductive Bible Study

On the surface, the inductive method sounds complicated. It's not. In-depth is a better way to describe it. But, when it comes down to it, the inductive approach only has three primary steps:

1. **Observation:** What does the Bible say?
2. **Interpretation:** What does the Bible mean?
3. **Application:** How does the Bible apply to your life?

First, you observe the text before you interpret it. Then, once you've rightly interpreted the text, you can make appropriate application to your life.

Let's start with observation.

Observation

The first step is observing and engaging with the text. You are looking at the text and asking questions, but not making any conclusions. The goal is figuring out what you need to learn to interpret the passage. There are five ways you should observe Scripture.

Step 1: Compare Translations

One of the easiest ways to observe the text is by reading it in multiple translations. Read it multiple times in your preferred Bible, and then compare it to other translations.

As you make comparisons, you may find that one translation makes it easier to understand the passage than another. Or, you might find interesting notes about how the various translations chose to translate key words or phrases.

Make notes of key differences between the translations and what stands out in each.

Step 2: Ask Questions

The key to engaging the text in a thoughtful manner is asking the right questions. It's like sitting in a classroom lecture. As you listen to the professor, your mind engages the information, which allows you to then ask questions that further enhance your understanding of the material. When you study the Bible you're "listening" to it as you observe and ask questions that will lead to a right interpretation.

In their book *Inductive Bible Study*, Fuhr and Köstenberger cite four kinds of interpretive questions we should ask when observing the text.

1. **Questions of Content:** What is the substance of the text and the significance of the content? Who, what, where, and when are the questions you want to ask here.

2. **Questions of Relationship:** What is the relationship between words, phrases, and concepts within and between literary units. How does the text relate to other areas of Scripture, both near and far?

3. **Questions of Intention:** What is the author's intent? There is always a reason why an author wrote what he did and how he said it. Your questions here help you ponder the *why*.

4. **Questions of Implication:** What are the implications and ramifications of various interpretations? What inferences can be made based on what is happening in the text? How will a given interpretation impact the rest of Scripture?[5]

Write these questions in your notebook. Don't try to answer them, just note the questions you want answered.

Step 3: Find Key Words

As you observe the text, words and phrases should begin to stand out. You want to note these words because they may help you in your interpretation. Questions like these will help you find these words:

- Are there words significant within the context?
- Do words repeat? Are there synonyms?
- Are there words that may have theological significance?
- Does the text mention unfamiliar places or things?
- Are there figures of speech or symbols?

Only make note of these words. You will investigate them later.

Step 4: Observe Literary Features

The fourth step looks for literary features as you observe the text. Look for things like repetition, comparison and contrast, conjunctions, illustrations, and the like. Are there figures of speech? Does the author use a certain tone?

Highlight or underline such phrases in your Bible. Connect the points and visualize how the passage fits together. Mark repeated words, phrases, or ideas. Be attentive and look for any associations and observations you can find in the text.

---

[5]Fuhr, R. A., Jr., & Köstenberger, A. J. (2016). *Inductive Bible study: Observation, interpretation, and application through the lenses of history, literature, and theology.* Nashville, TN: B&H Academic, pp. 77-83.

Step 5: Analyze the Structure

For the final step, examine the structure of the passage. It may not seem obvious, but these details can help you make better interpretations.

First, recognize the genre. From there, look for any key segments and ways to break up the text.

- What are the boundaries where thoughts begin and end?
- Is the text structured to convey a certain message?

When you understand the structure and genre of the text, it is easier to understand the language and other components used by the author, which ultimately informs your interpretation.

Interpretation

With your observation complete, you can begin your interpretation of the text. In this step you will investigate the text based on the questions you asked during observation. You will answer questions by letting the text reveal itself. You are still not making any conclusions about the text's meaning. Like observation, interpretation includes five steps. Let's look at each step in order.

Step 1: Consider the Context

First, consider the context. Look at the passage and place it in its proper boundaries. At this point, keep in mind the triad of history, literature, and theology. Using this interpretive triad, here's how each context helps interpretation.

History

- What is the geopolitical context? Is there anything significant going on in the world at this time as it relates to this text?
- What aspects of culture do you need to keep in mind?
- What are the setting, situation, and occasion for this writing?

Literature

- Where does this fall in Scripture? Is it Old or New Testament?
- What section of the New or Old Testament is it contained in?
- What is the genre and/or sub-genre?

- How does the passage relate to what precedes and follows?
- What is the main idea of the passage?

Theology
- What key themes are presented in the text?
- What covenants are in place at the time when the passage is written? How does this impact the text?
- How does the passage relate to the overarching meta narrative of the gospel?

These questions get to the heart of the circumstances surrounding the passage and where it fits in the Bible and history in general.

Step 2: Compare Scripture with Scripture
As you learned in week 2 (pg. 23), the best way to interpret Scripture is to allow it to interpret itself. The second step of interpretation is doing just that. Do a cross-reference study of the passage.

Step 3: Word Studies
Understanding the meaning of words and phrases will help your interpretation. To get this information you must do word studies, which you learned how to do in week 6 of this workbook (pg. 111).

Step 4: Topical Studies
The fourth step looks at the whole of Scripture to understand its teaching on a given subject. Topical studies will help you to this end, which you learned in week 4 (pg. 65).

Step 5: Consult Other Resources
Up to this point in the inductive process, you have consulted few resources. You've only used resources that give you general background on Scripture and lexicons that define words. You have not yet touched resources like commentaries and study Bibles. Now is the time to bring those resources into your study.

These resources should enhance your study of Scripture. They also have the added benefit of double checking your work. While Bible study is highly personal, you do not study in isolation from the rest of church history and the Body of Christ. You should lean on your brothers and sisters in the faith to help you understand God's Word. This is why you should, as a last step of interpretation, consult the works of others.

After you've completed this step, you should have an understanding of what the passage says and how it relates to the rest of Scripture.

Application

Application is the final step of the inductive Bible study method. God spoke to his people when he wrote the Bible. He continues to speak today through those same words. Because God speaks through his word, it is important to know how to apply what the Bible says. You can do this in two steps.

Step 1: Establish the Relevance

When studying Scripture, you will quickly learn that making application can prove quite difficult. This is partly due to the Bible being an old book, which makes it hard to figure out how it relates to the present day. So, you must determine its relevance before seeking application. Do this by evaluating the text & asking questions like:

- What was the author's intent in writing?
- What was the application for the original audience?
- Is the text relaying a narrative or teaching?
- What is the underlying principle of the text?
- Based on that principle, how does it relate to today?
- How can you apply this text?

Asking questions like this helps you make appropriate application.

Step 2: Make it Personal

Knowledge without application is meaningless. The application's second step moves you beyond head knowledge by making the text personal. Here, you rely wholly on the Holy Spirit to guide you, asking him to reveal how the passage directly relates to your life.

There are no guidelines for how this should take place. But, it does require thought and intentionality. Ask how the passage and application impacts you. How is the Holy Spirit moving you to respond to the passage? From there, meditate on Scripture and put the application into action, much like the final steps of the H.E.A.R.T. journaling method from week 1 (pg. 1).

Summarize Your Findings

Once you've completed all three steps of the inductive method, the final step is to summarize your findings. You should be able to write a few sentence summary of what the passage is about and how it relates to your life. Summarizing the text is a good exercise to help solidify the passage and its application in your own heart and mind.

A Surefire Bible Study Method

Inductive Bible study is a surefire method for getting the most out of your time in God's Word. The steps are simple: 1) observe, 2) interpret, and 3) apply. If there's one Bible study method you implement, inductive Bible study should be it. It's a one-stop shop for studying God's Word.

So, if you're ready to put it into practice, turn the page and begin the final two weeks of exercises.

Observation

1. Compare Translations

2. Ask Questions

3. Find Key Words

4. Observe Literary Features

5. Analyze the Structure

Interpretation

1. Consider the Context

2. Compare Scripture with Scripture

3. Word Studies

4. Topical Studies

5. Consult Other Resources

Application

1. Establish the Relevance

2. Make it Personal

Summarize Your Study

Example Exercise

2 Thessalonians 1:5-12

Note: Due to the depth of the inductive Bible study method, the notes below are slightly abbreviated, and in some areas show summaries of the work, such as in the word study section of interpretation.

Observation

Step 1: Compare Translations
Bible translations used: ESV, CSB, NLT, NIV, NASB, NKJV

Compared to the ESV, translations like the CSB and NLT are much easier to read and understand the flow of what's being said in the text. There is less ambiguity & woodenness in the translation, especially in making sense of the first few verses and what Paul is trying to say. There was not much in the other translations that helped make better sense of the passage.

General observations:
- Be sure to not take this passage in isolation from the verses that come before it, as it provides significant context, particularly in what is being spoken of in verse 5.
- We are considered worthy of the kingdom of God through our suffering and perseverance in the faith
- Yet, our persecution and suffering by God's enemies is not going unnoticed; God's judgment will come upon them at his Second Coming
- God's judgment is righteous, not just something that he does on a whim or without any standard of measurement

- Paul's prayer at the end of this section is that God would work in these believers to put in their hearts to do the good works that he desires for them to do so that Christ might be glorified in them
  - These works are done IN FAITH and by HIS POWER
  - As we glorify Christ in these works, he also glorifies us

Step 2: Ask Questions
- What exactly does it mean to be "considered worthy" (v. 5) and "may make you worthy" (v. 11)?
- How/why is it just for God to repay those who have afflicted us? (I think I already know the answer to this, but want to investigate it more)
- What does it mean to "obey the gospel" in this context? (v. 8)
- How does God grant relief to the afflicted?
- What is meant by "eternal destruction," since we are not talking annihilationism?
- What is the glory of God's might?
- How is God/Christ glorified in his saints at the Second Coming?
- How are we glorified by Christ in doing good works?
- Why are the Thessalonians being afflicted & facing suffering?
- How are we made worthy of God's calling?

Step 3: Find Key Words
- Do some study on suffering, affliction, and afflict
- Is there anything unique/peculiar about the word "repay" in verse 6?

Step 4: Observe Literary Features
- Lots of repetition & contrast between those who are being afflicted & those doing the afflicting.
- Synonyms = affliction, suffering
- Synonyms = judgment, destruction, punishment

- Overall idea seems to be the encouragement of believers that those who afflict them will face judgment by God

Step 5: Analyze the Structure
- This section is bookended by talk of being found worthy with judgment of the wicked sandwiched between
- This section is mostly self contained:
  Before - opening & greeting
  After - new subject about concerns surrounding the Lord's coming

Interpretation

Step 1: Consider the Context

Historical Context: Thessalonica is a prominent city in the Roman empire that sits on one of the major travel routes. There is a significant Jewish population, as Paul preached in the synagogue during his visit to the city (Acts 17). There was significant opposition from the Jews who did not believe the message Paul preached, setting the city in an uproar.

Literary Context: 2 Thessalonians is the second letter Paul wrote to this church. It is a New Testament epistle (letter) and is likely one of his earlier letters. The focus of the letter is answering questions this church has about the timing of Christ's return.

This passage speaks specifically about suffering and how God will handle it. It comes right after opening the letter and before answering their questions about Christ's coming.

Theological Context: The overall theme of the letter is Christ's return and how it relates to Christians. As believers, the return of Christ is our hope, so these are details we want to be aware of.

As it relates to this passage, suffering is also a part of the Christian life (2 Timothy 2:3). This passage should encourage us that God sees and is aware of what is happening, and the offenders will not go unpunished.

Step 2: Compare Scripture with Scripture
How/why is it just for God to repay those who have afflicted us? (I think I already know the answer to this, but want to investigate it more)

- God judges impartially and will judge people according to their deeds (Deut. 10:17; Ps. 98:9; Rom. 2:9; Col. 3:25; 1 Pet. 1:17).
- God is an enemy to those who oppress & oppose his children (Ex. 23:22; Deut. 32:41-43; Zech. 2:8; Rev. 6:10; 11:18; 16:5, 6; 18:20, 24; 19:2).
- For the believer, we do not fall under God's judgment because we are his children and Christ has already born the wrath for our sins against God, whereas we are imputed with his righteousness (Rom. 4:7-8, 11, 23-24; 2 Cor. 5:21; Phil. 3:9). Not only are we avoiding judgment because of our faith, but those without faith & persecute God's children are judged.

Steps 3 & 4: Topical & Word Studies
Do some study on suffering, affliction, and afflict (have I studied these words before?)

- suffering - paschō #G3958 - 42x - suffer/endure (Phil. 1:29; 1 Thess. 2:14; 1 Pet. 2:21; 4:19). Particularly, this can be suffering at the hands of others
- affliction - thlipsis #G2347 - 45x - trouble that inflicts distress, oppression, affliction, tribulation. This word was used in v. 4 to describe the affliction believers endured, now the tables are turned & those who afflicted Christians are being afflicted by God. Also, this is translated as "tribulation," which is the same word to describe the terror at Christ's Second Coming, so there is much detail concerning how they will be afflicted.

- afflict - thlibō #G2346 - 10x - to cause to be troubled. Used in back-2-back verses, 1st for the bad people, 2nd (v. 7) for the believers. For believers, this is something they should expect (2 Cor. 1:6; 4:8; 7:5; 1 Thess. 3:4; Heb. 11:37). Unbelievers should expect affliction too, but they don't.
  - The overarching use of this word is in relation to the Christian and their suffering and how they ought to endure such trials. DO NOT LOSE THIS FOCUS!
  - In the context of this passage, we are indeed talking about the affliction of the unrighteous and the punishment they will suffer, but it comes as payment for their affliction of believers. It's their righteous judgment.

Is there anything unique/peculiar about the word "repay" in verse 6?

- antapodidōmi #G467 - 7x - to practice reciprocity with respect to an obligation or to exact retribution
- Two key passages where this word is used fit into the context of this passage: Rom. 12:19; Heb. 10:30.
- Nothing particularly special about this word, it means what it means. Comes from the root word didōmi (to give [used 415x])
- See related cognate word apodidōmi (#G591 - 48x). Matt. 12:36; 16:27; Rom. 2:6; 2 Tim. 4:14; Rev. 22:12.

What does it mean to "obey the gospel" in this context? (v. 8)

- hupakouō #G5219 - 21x - to follow instructions
- comes from the root word akouō (to hear)
- Rom. 6:16; 10:16; 2 Thess. 3:14; Heb. 11:8; Acts 5:32.
- In this context, it would appear that these people have heard the gospel and refused obeying it, thus they are being punished accordingly.

How is God/Christ glorified in his saints at the Second Coming?

- endoxazomai #G1740 - 2x - to be the object of great honor
- In the context, he is glorified because of our faith/belief in the gospel. Those who glorify & marvel at him are the ones who have believed.
- His Second Coming is the day that we've long awaited, and we are going to rejoice when that day finally arrives because: 1) we will see him face-to-face, 2) our suffering and affliction will be over, and 3) the wicked will finally be judged

How are we glorified by Christ in doing good works?

- The name of Christ is glorified in us when we do the good works that he has prepared for us and as we grow in sanctification, because we are walking worthy of the calling by which we've been called. In essence, he's glorified in us because we are living as he desires for us to live.
- As stated in earlier verses, we glorify Christ through our faith and obedience.
- This is reciprocal in nature. We glorify him with our lives and he continually glorifies himself in us through the working of the Spirit in our lives.

Step 5: Consult Other Resources
What is the glory of God's might?

- This phrase is in parallel with "the presence of the Lord" so that the two phrases are expressing the same thing
- There is also a parallelism in verse 8 with "those who do not know God" and "those who do not obey the gospel..." (there may be subtle distinction here, but they are roughly parallel).
- This phrase and verse parallels Isaiah's words in Isa. 2:10, 19, 21 (found in the New Testament Use of the Old Testament).
- This phrase also shows the greatest punishment of hell, which is being completely cast away from God's presence & grace for all eternity.

- This phrase is also quoted & used in the Westminster Confession of Faith (Chapter 33, 2)

Application

Step 1: Establish the Relevance
Paul wrote to alleviate the concerns of the Thessalonians about missing the Lord's return and to keep them focused on daily serving the Lord, even in the midst of suffering. The Thessalonians should keep doing what they're doing because God sees all that is happening. They will be blessed for their good, and their opponents will be judged for their mistreatment.

Christians today face suffering all over the world, and we should have a similar response to the Thessalonians. We ought to keep doing good, knowing that God will reward our good works and will give us eternal rest. And we can also rest knowing our enemies will not go unpunished in this world, all while we pray for their salvation.

Step 2: Make it Personal
Personally, I have to realize suffering is inevitable in this world. I must daily pray to God for the strength to stand strong for the gospel and doing the good he has already prepared for me to do. I cannot worry about the opposition that comes my way, but when it does, I know I have the strength in Christ to endure.

Summarize
The name of God will be glorified in believers because they prove themselves worthy of the name "Christian." Even in the midst of suffering, believers continue to stand firm in the faith & do good, which is a testimony of God's Spirit within us. And we can press forward, knowing that God has not turned a blind eye to evil, but will judge it in his time, at his Second Coming.

Workbook Exercises

Note: Because of the depth of the inductive Bible study method, there is only one passage to study for the week. Take your time and work through each step in the inductive method over the course of the week. The final week, week 8, is a second week of exercises in the inductive method.

Week 1
Galatians 5:16-26

Week 2
James 1:19-27

Appendix 1: 5 Things to Pray Before You Open Your Bible

When I was younger, while in a haste to complete my time in the Word, prayer was something I would often neglect. This resulted in lots of unfruitful time in the Word where I walked away scratching my head with little to transform my life. It wasn't until years later that I realized how important prayer is to Bible study.

We often forget that Bible study is a spiritual experience where we commune with God. Too often we approach it from an academic point of view. Instead of fellowshipping with God, we only seek head knowledge or to check a box. Yet, God speaks through the Bible's pages, because they are literally his words. Therefore, we need to come prepared when we study his Word. Prayer is the primary means by which this takes place.

With that in mind, here are five things you should pray before you begin any time of Bible study.

1. Pray for Forgiveness of Sins

Before you open your Bible, you must first repent of your sins. Without fail, between the last time you studied until the next, you have fallen short of God's standard. If you're anything like me, you probably sinned with a stray thought in the time it took to walk to your desk. We have all become such experts at sinning that we fail to realize how often we commit the crime.

It's foolish to think God will bless your time of study if you are unrepentant of sin. Be cleansed of your sin and come to the table ready for a feast. Ask him to forgive you of any and all sins you've committed. This prayer guarantees you are walking in fellowship with the Holy Spirit, the one who teaches and explains all biblical truth.

2. Ask God to Speak

Once you've repented and are in fellowship with God, you then need to ask for the Holy Spirit's help. Bible study is about letting God speak through his Word. As such, it would be foolish to not ask him to commune with you in your study. The unfortunate truth is it's possible to read the Bible all day and walk away with zero to show for it.

I've read the Bible too many times & failed to ask God to speak. Those are the times I walked away asking myself, "What did I just read?" Don't let that be you. Pray for God to speak to you through his holy Scriptures.

3. Pray for Focus

There's nothing worse than wasting time, especially during Bible study. With jam-packed schedules, there is only so much time to spend with God in Scripture each day. You must make the most of your time. In your prayers, ask God to keep distraction at bay so you can focus on his Word alone.

Speaking from experience, when I don't pray this prayer, my mind is prone to wander or gets caught up in details that don't matter. When this happens my time is squandered and I don't come away uplifted. Yet, when I ask for focus, the Lord is faithful to answer that prayer. Sure, I still have to fight to stay focused, but the battle isn't nearly as hard as when I don't seek his help.

Pro Tip: Keep pen and paper nearby. When random thoughts, like needing to buy milk, enter your mind, write them down and continue with your study. This frees up your brain from trying to remember such details, which can otherwise prove to be a distraction.

4. Seek Clarity

One goal of Bible study is understanding what you've read. Why not ask God for clarity? This is a prayer God is pleased to answer because he wants us to grow in our knowledge of the faith. Bible study is hard work, so it's worth asking God to make it a little bit easier for us. This prayer doesn't mean the answers will jump off the page (although it sometimes happens that way); but, what it does mean is that as you put in the work God will help you make sense of it all.

Now, there are times when God doesn't answer this prayer, and that's okay too. There are many times you'll want to understand a passage or topic only to remain flustered. Sometimes God doesn't want you to understand something yet. Often times it's to keep you humble. But, when you come back to the same subject at a later date, praying the same prayer, God does answer and you're blessed because of it. Sometimes he even reveals the reasons why he withheld understanding in times past.

Nevertheless, prayer for clarity is vital if you want to get the most out of your Bible study.

5. Pray for Application

Lastly, pray for the application of the things you're studying. Head knowledge alone is not enough. You must take everything to heart so it can transform your life. This is when the Bible comes to life. Real growth only happens when you live out what you've learned.

For me, this is the hardest part of Bible study, so I always ask God to help me apply his Word to my life.

Do not neglect praying for application.

Remember to Pray

If you remember to pray for these five things before your times of study, I trust you will walk away fulfilled.

Make it a habit to pray before you open your Bible. It doesn't have to be a long prayer, but make sure you do it.

Appendix 2: How to Build a Bible Study Library

When it comes to building a Bible study library, there is lots of advice out there. Some people tell you to stick with the free stuff. Others recommend spending hundreds or thousands of dollars on books or Bible software. Which way is right? Is there a wrong way to build a Bible study library?

In a way, they are both right. And yes, there is a wrong way to build a library. But, I will show you how to build a Bible study library you can be proud of.

Library Building Principles

Before you start building your Bible study library, there are a few principles you should know first. These are lessons I have learned as I built my own library over the years.

1. Large libraries are often wasted

Bible software companies like to put lots of books in their packages. These companies want their packages to have as many books as possible so it appears you are getting more for your money. They will even tell you that a larger library will make your Bible study better. Truth be told, many of the books in a large library will never get used or read. You end up buying books you think you might use one day, but you eventually forget you own it. Don't waste money on stuff you think you might use; only buy what you know you will use.

2. Content is duplicated

There's not a lot of new or innovative content. It's standard practice that commentaries quote & refer to one another, with most coming to the same conclusions. Dictionaries do similar, with similar entries being found across dictionaries. If you're going to own multiple resources, like a commentary, I recommend purchasing across doctrinal and denominational lines if you want varying viewpoints.

3. Focus on the essentials

There are literally thousands of Bible study resources available for purchase. But just because a book is available doesn't mean you need it in your library. Evaluate every study tool before you add it to your library. Will it help you achieve your goals? Does it say the same thing as another resource you own? If it's not adding value, you don't need it. Even if it's a great deal, if it's not something you want to study, it's a wasted purchase.

4. The best tools are the ones you use

All in all, the most important principle is this: the best tools are the ones you use. Much like the best Bible translation is the one you read, the best Bible tools are the ones you are most familiar with and use on a regular basis.

How to Build a Bible Study Library

When it comes to building a Bible study library, my best advice is this: keep it simple.

You don't need to spend thousands of dollars building a grand theological library. Instead, examine the Bible study resources available to you and only add the ones that add value.

When I help people build their Bible study libraries, I always recommend starting with three items and building from there as needed. The three items are:

- Study Bible
- Full Bible commentary
- Bible Dictionary

Study Bible

Study Bibles are great because they are an all-in-one resource. You get your Bible text, some commentary, introductions, and a wealth of other tools.

My favorite Study Bible is the *ESV Study Bible* from Crossway. This is one of the most comprehensive Study Bibles on the market today. Nearly a decade later and few others have come close to competing with it. It has everything you need and then some.

My second recommendation is the *CSB Disciple's Study Bible* from Holman Bibles. It may not be as robust as the previous Bible, but I love its focus on discipleship. The notes are geared toward helping a young believer understand how Scripture relates to daily living, while still providing the essentials for deeper study.

Full Bible Commentary

Full Bible commentaries are designed for all Christians and cover the Bible in its entirety. While these commentaries may not be as thorough as their single-book counterparts, the editors take care in explaining any difficult passages.

Of all the single volume commentaries on the market, the two I recommend are the *New Bible Commentary* and the *Expositor's Bible Commentary: Abridged Edition*. Both commentaries do an excellent job explaining the text of Scripture. Comparing the two, *Expositor's* is a bit more comprehensive as it's actually two books (Old and New Testament), whereas the *New Bible Commentary* is a single volume & about half the total number of pages. Breadth aside, either gets the job done.

Bible Dictionary

Commentaries and Study Bibles are great at explaining the text of the Bible, but they don't always go into detail about some of the concepts and words used. This is where a good Bible Dictionary comes into play. Bible Dictionaries are, in effect, encyclopedias for the Bible.

When it comes to picking a Bible Dictionary, there are two I recommend: the *Essential Bible Dictionary* and the *New Bible Dictionary*. Your choice of dictionary will largely depend on your budget and needs.

The *Essential Bible Dictionary* is smaller and its definitions are more succinct. This one reads more like a dictionary than an encyclopedia, but it still gives you all the vital information you need. One benefit is that it does contain full color images & maps, which can be helpful in your studies. It's perfect for answering your questions & quickly getting you back to your study.

The *New Bible Dictionary* is a good bit larger and contains more in-depth entries than you'll find in the above dictionary. If you're more the curious type this is the one you'll want. It's an A to Z of Bible terms, place names, books, people and doctrine. Plus, it's recognized by many as an essential reference work.

Start Your Library Today

These three items may not seem like much, but they provide the necessary foundation for accurately handling the Word of God. From there, consider investing in Bible software. Research and find the one that works best for you, and then buy what you need & will use. Don't fall for the trick that having more books will help you study better.

Even if you don't have a lot of money, you can get started without breaking the bank. You can even start for free like I did with tools like Olive Tree and websites like Blue Letter Bible.

Just know you don't need to spend thousands of dollars to understand the Bible. As long as you have a few solid tools, you'll have what you need to learn and apply God's Word.

If you do choose to invest in Bible software, check page 205 for two great deals.

Appendix 3: How to Pick the Perfect Study Bible

If you walk into your local Christian bookstore and head over to the Bibles section, you're sure to be inundated with the selection of study Bibles. With so many to choose from and sometimes with a hefty price tag to boot, how do you know which study Bible is right for you? That's a good question.

Here's what you should look for when choosing a study Bible.

What Makes for a Good Study Bible?

The key to a good study Bible is that it contains the right components. You should be able to use it for the majority of your study needs and have it be your first line of defense in answering questions about Scripture. So, a good study Bible needs to be well-rounded and do a lot of things well. It should be an all-in-one resource for Bible study.

People made fun of the *ESV Study Bible* when it was first published because it was massive. Carrying it around was a workout. Yet, its size can be attributed to it being a comprehensive Bible study tool. If it was the only tool a person owned, Crossway wanted to make sure it was a good one. And that it was and still is!

Now let's see what makes up a well-rounded study Bible.

Study Notes

Aside from the Bible text, study notes are the most important element in a study Bible. If the goal is to understand the Bible, the notes must help you toward that end. So, look for a Bible with extensive notes that explain the passage. Flip throughout the Bible and see how in-depth (or sparse) the notes are. The more elaborate the notes the better.

Book Introductions

When studying a new book of the Bible, you must get acquainted with it. Like meeting a new friend, you need to make proper introductions. You need to do the same when you study the Bible. This typically involves finding out lots of background information. Book introductions go a long way in helping with this.

Good book introductions will provide the following:

- A summary of the book
- The genre(s)
- The author & date
- Key themes, people, and places

Additionally, you may find information such as: how the book fits into the Bible's overarching narrative, literary features, key passages, the purpose & occasion for the book, a timeline, and so on.

By time you're done reading the introduction, you should have a broad understanding of the book of the Bible you're about to study.

Outlines

The book's introduction will often include an outline showing the book's structure. These are invaluable. At a glance you can see: 1) how long the book is, 2) major divisions in the text, and 3) the flow of the narrative or topic. The outline is like an aerial view of the entire forest before walking through it.

Outlines can help you plan your study strategy. It can help you decide how large a portion of Scripture you want to tackle at a given time and determine how long it will take to study a book or section. After reading the introduction, outlines are the next stop on the study train. And my philosophy is this: the more detailed the outline the better.

Maps

Any study Bible worth its weight should have maps, preferably color ones. The biblical narrative involves lots of movement and place names. If you're not familiar with the geography it's easy to find yourself confused, not knowing what's happening in the text. Maps help you figure out what's going on and where everything is.

Sure, most Bibles have five or six maps in the back, but a good study Bible has maps throughout the study notes. For example, Joshua's conquest of the Promised Land is quite involved. To keep yourself properly oriented to all the activity, the *ESV Study Bible* inserts several maps throughout the book to illustrate what's happening and where, along with arrows showing routes of travel.

Often overlooked, the number & quality of maps should play an important role in your decision making process when purchasing a study Bible.

Charts

The Bible contains a lot of information and sometimes it's difficult to make sense of it all. This is why any good study Bible will use charts & tables to lay out key data.

What kind of information am I talking about? Things like: chronologies & timelines, calendars, the kings of Israel & Judah, Jesus' parables & miracles, the sermons in Acts, and the spiritual gifts, just to name a few. Yes, you could piece this information together yourself, but charts make your Bible study more productive.

Concordance

A concordance is essential for your study Bible. Thankfully, just about every Bible these days has some level of a concordance in the back.

Your concordance is your assistant when searching for a word in the Bible and you don't know where it's located. It's also the first tool in line when starting a topical or word study.

While it should be a given, make sure your study Bible has one before buying it. If it doesn't, you've been cheated!

Articles & Essays

The last thing to look for in a study Bible is its additional features. Most study Bibles now include additional articles and essays to help deepen your faith. While not essential, these can become a vital asset to your spiritual growth.

What kinds of things should you look for? Here's a sample of what you can find in a few study Bibles:

- *CSB Disciple's Study Bible* — the back of this study Bible contains articles on discipleship and discipleship groups
- *Key Word Study Bible* — a condensed Strong's dictionary and other word study tools are contained in the back
- *Reformation Study Bible* — here you will find historic creeds & confessions, catechisms, and articles on Christian living

Again, while not essential, they are certainly useful for study, especially if this is your primary (or only) study tool. You can never go wrong with additional resources for Bible study and maturing in your faith.

The Dangers of Study Bibles

For all the good that study Bibles offer, these are two things you should also keep at the forefront of you mind when making your purchase.

Theological Bias

Study Bibles tend to fall into one of two camps: they either try to be mainline evangelical or have a denominational or theological emphasis. Therefore, as best you can, you need to figure out where any given study Bible lands on that spectrum.

You do not want to purchase a study Bible that contradicts what you or your church believes the Bible to teach. For example, if you do not believe in the continuation of the miraculous spiritual gifts (miracles, speaking in tongues, etc.) then you would not want to purchase the *Fire Bible* or the *New Spirit Filled Life Bible* which promote such beliefs. Likewise, if you're not Reformed you'd want to stay away from the *Reformation Heritage KJV Study Bible*.

Here are things to look for that will help you figure out a study Bible's theological bias.

- Look for catch phrases or key words in the title (i.e. reformation, fire, spirit filled, orthodox, etc.)
- Check the editor, contributors & endorsements — like key words, it's easy to figure out the theological bias when you know who wrote or promotes it
- Check the publisher — a handful of publishers have a clear doctrinal position based on their history & often publish in that vein
- Finally, without any clear indication, assume it takes a balanced evangelical approach — this is the position of *most* study Bibles

Not All Study Bibles Are Created Equal

Last, consider that not all study Bibles are created equal. Each study Bible has its strengths & weaknesses and these need to be considered. Many specialized study Bibles can be sparse on notes (or have none at all), but heavy on articles & devotions. For example, the *Hebrew-Greek Key Word Study Bible* is very light on study notes because of its emphasis on word studies. Yet, the *ESV Study Bible* is balanced & does just about everything well.

My Favorite Study Bibles

Now that you know what to look for in a study Bible, here are a few I recommend and use regularly in my own studies.

- ESV Study Bible
- Gospel Transformation Study Bible
- Biblical Theology Study Bible (formerly the NIV Zondervan Study Bible)
- Reformation Study Bible (2015 edition)
- Life Application Study Bible
- CSB Disciple's Study Bible

Everyone has their own preferences, and the same is true for study Bibles; so, choose the one that ticks the right boxes and meets your study needs.

Appendix 4: Biblical Meditation

Picture it. You're sitting on your living room floor. Legs folded, eyes closed, palms facing upward with index fingers & thumbs touching as they rest on your knees. Now you hear the chant, "Ohmmmm....," as you clear your mind and seek a deeper connection with your inner self. This is what comes to mind for most when discussing the topic of meditation. That is one of many forms of meditation; but, did you know there's such a thing as biblical meditation?

Yes, biblical meditation is a thing. Unfortunately, the modern church has forgotten and neglected its practice. When the world pushed in with its forms of meditation, the church's got pushed aside. It's gotten to the point that when you mention meditation in the church it's something that looks eerily similar to the world, or you get shunned altogether for wanting to bring something worldly into the house of God. This is not what God wants; he wants us to practice meditation, but he wants us to do it his way.

So let me introduce you to the practice of biblical meditation. In doing so, I hope you will see its benefit for your spiritual life. The material is adapted from David Saxton's excellent book on the subject titled *God's Battle Plan for the Mind: The Puritan Practice of Biblical Meditation*.

Let's begin with a definition.

What is Biblical Meditation?

The world has muddied the definition of what it means to meditate, so we must be clear and deliberate in defining "biblical meditation." To do this, let's look at what it is and isn't.

What It's Not

As we describe what biblical mediation is not, we begin with the church. Within Christendom, there are several movements that encourage mysticism and contemplative prayer. Through stillness and repetition of words & phrases, these forms of meditation seek an encounter and union with God. While both have been practiced for centuries, neither finds its foundation in the Word of God. Instead, they seek spiritual experience apart from the Bible. Within such practices you can attribute nearly anything that comes to mind as a word from the Lord. Inevitably, this means we attribute words to God that he never spoke, yet they are often given equal or greater weight than Scripture. That's dangerous!

At the other end of the spectrum are Transcendental Meditation and Far Eastern religions. In contemporary culture, these methods are taught as relaxation and stress relief techniques. By becoming a passive vessel and emptying one's mind, the practitioner focuses on inner awareness and connection with the universe. Much like mysticism & contemplative prayer, the center of thought becomes one's own imagination and reasoning, without basis in hard truth. A very real danger of such meditation is that emptying one's mind leaves it open for spiritual enemies to invade.

Additionally, biblical mediation is more than focusing your thoughts on a specific subject. Many promote the idea that we spend 10 to 15 minutes a day in silence, settling our mind, and finding one thing to think about. While this can prove helpful in some settings, it too is not biblical meditation.

What It Is

The best definitions for biblical meditation are found in Scripture.

In the Old Testament, there are two key Hebrew words translated as "meditate," they are *hagah* (Strong's H1897) & *siychah* (Strong's H7881). The first word connotes an "internal brooding over something in the heart." The latter involves lovingly going over things in one's mind. Both words have the heart and one's thoughts in view. Therefore, meditation is not a mindless or empty activity; it is an activity that engages the mind. Key passages where these words are used give us a picture of what biblical meditation looks like. A sampling includes: Joshua 1:8; Psalm 1:2; 119:97, 148.

Likewise, the concept of meditation is throughout the pages of the New Testament. The imagery is bountiful, using words like: dwelling, thinking, considering, pondering, setting one's mind, and remembering. No matter the word used, the idea is the same. As Christians, we are to constantly have the things of God before our mind so it can direct our lives. A sampling of passages for New Testament meditation include: Luke 2:19; Philippians 4:8; Colossians 3:2; Hebrews 10:24-25; 12:3; and Revelation 2:5.

The Puritans frequently taught on this subject, but I like Thomas Watson's definition of biblical meditation best. He writes, "Meditation... is a holy exercise of the mind whereby we bring the truth of God to remembrance, and do seriously ponder upon them and apply them to ourselves."

Types of Biblical Meditation

In their teaching on the practice of meditation, the Puritans put forth two types: deliberate and occasional.

Deliberate meditation is the most familiar; and, of the two, is by far the most important. Deliberate meditation is an intentional time set aside when one opens the Bible and studies it, pondering the truths of God, joining it with prayer. This time ought to be as regular as possible. Here the believer lingers on the truth of Scripture and applies it to his life. In other words, this is your normal time of Bible study.

Secondarily, you can practice occasional meditation several times throughout the day. This type of meditation compares everyday experiences to the truths of God's Word. With this practice you can transform mundane tasks and thoughts into opportunities for spiritual pondering. Proverbs 6:6 illustrates the concept when Solomon taught diligence in work by looking at the habits of ants. Everyday moments can point us to God's Word and how it applies to our life. This is the type of meditation encouraged in the H.E.A.R.T. journaling method (pg. 1).

Both types of meditation are beneficial to the life of the believer and provide opportunity to think about heavenly truths at any time.

How to Meditate

The quickest way to dive into biblical meditation is to start with what you're already doing in your Bible study.

When you start, ask for the Holy Spirit's help. Without his assistance, your Bible study and meditation will be fruitless. When you petition him, your prayer should be for clarity in understanding, as well as the mental capacity to restrain distraction. Both tasks are easier when distraction is kept at bay.

With prayer in place, turn to your text of Scripture. Biblical meditation is not to be done apart from God's Word. As you study the Bible each day, **highlight a verse or two that stand out above the rest**. Make note of it so you can refer to it later.

One key way to meditate on any given verse is to **examine how it applies to your life**. Sometimes this is an easy process; yet, other times it can take a bit longer to figure out how God desires you to change through his Word. Application should be a regular part of your Bible study. You should have some level of application before you walk away from your time of study. All of this is part of deliberate meditation.

Now, as you go about your day, occasional meditation kicks in. **Use free moments in your day to ponder the words and meaning of the verse(s) that stood out in your study.** The moments of your day are ripe for spiritual application and seeing the beauty of God's Word at work.

Finally, thank God for it all. He is the one that allows and helps you meditate on his Word. In all, **your days should both begin and end with prayer & thanksgiving.**

That's how you meditate!

Put Biblical Meditation into Practice

We've all practiced biblical meditation in one form or another. Now that you know what it is, be more deliberate and occasional in your meditation. Don't let a day go by without meditating on God's Word.

As Scripture says, "Man does not live by bread alone, but man lives by every word that comes from the mouth of the Lord" (Deuteronomy 8:3).

Note: all quotations are from *God's Battle Plan for the Mind: The Puritan Practice of Biblical Meditation* by David Saxton.

Appendix 5: Additional Passages for Study

If you find that you need more practice working through a given Bible study method, use these passages for additional study.

Week 1: Bible Journaling
- Numbers 6
- Revelation 4:1-11
- Psalm 95
- John 1:35-51
- Galatians 2:15-3:14

Week 2: Cross-References
- Genesis 3:1-5
- 1 John 5:1-5
- Exodus 19:1-6
- Colossians 1:15-18
- Galatians 4:1-7

Week 3: Bible Survey
- 1 John
- 2 Thessalonians
- Obadiah
- Ruth
- James

Week 4: Topical Study
- Pride
- Doubt
- Fellowship
- Self Control
- Time

Week 5: Character Study
- Cain
- Hezekiah
- Jonah
- Naomi
- Jonathan

Week 6: Word Study
Read the passage & find a word to study

- 1 Thessalonians 4
- Matthew 13
- Genesis 1
- Psalm 45
- 2 Corinthians 1

Weeks 7 & 8: Inductive Bible Study
- Psalm 4
- Proverbs 1:1-7
- John 10:1-21
- 1 Corinthians 15:1-19
- Mark 10:46-52

Appendix 6: Foundations 260 Bible Reading Plan

Foundations 260 (F-260) is a Bible reading plan developed by Replicate Ministries. This is a 260-day Bible reading plan. Its purpose is to highlight the foundational passages of Scripture that all Christians should know. Many plans focus on reading the entire Bible in a year; not so with this plan. Instead, F-260 gives you the Bible's big picture without getting bogged down in the minor details.

Why only 260 days? F-260 isn't about checking off boxes. The goal isn't to say you read the Bible, but for you to digest and internalize it. This plan wants you to grow your faith. Therefore, this 52-week plan only has 5 readings each week. This gives you the weekends off for reflection, or catching up if you fall behind.

Each day's reading is only a chapter or two in length, instead of the handful required to read through the entire Bible in a year. This makes it easier to spend quality time in God's Word, instead of reading and quickly moving on. Joined with HEART journaling, it is a great way to study Scripture.

In addition, the plan includes memory verses that coincide with what you read each week.

The Foundations 260 Bible reading plan was developed by Replicate Ministries (replicate.org) and is used by permission.

WEEK 1
- Genesis 1-2
- Genesis 3-4
- Genesis 6-7
- Genesis 8-9
- Job 1-2

MEMORY VERSES:
Genesis 1:27
Hebrews 11:7

WEEK 2
- Job 38-39
- Job 40-42
- Genesis 11-12
- Genesis 15
- Genesis 16-17

MEMORY VERSES:
Hebrews 11:6, 8-10

WEEK 3
- Genesis 18-19
- Genesis 20-21
- Genesis 22
- Genesis 24
- Genesis 25:19-34; 26

MEMORY VERSES:
Romans 4:20-22
Hebrews 11:17-19

WEEK 4
- Genesis 27-28
- Genesis 29-30:24
- Genesis 31-32
- Genesis 33; 35
- Genesis 37

MEMORY VERSES:
2 Corinthians 10:12
1 John 3:18

WEEK 5
- Genesis 39-40
- Genesis 41
- Genesis 42-43
- Genesis 44-45
- Genesis 46-47

MEMORY VERSES:
Romans 8:28-30
Ephesians 3:20-21

WEEK 6
- Genesis 48-49
- Genesis 50-Exodus 1
- Exodus 2-3
- Exodus 4-5
- Exodus 6-7

MEMORY VERSES:
Genesis 50:20
Hebrews 11:24-26

WEEK 7
- Exodus 8-9
- Exodus 10-11
- Exodus 12
- Exodus 13:17-14
- Exodus 16-17

MEMORY VERSES:
John 1:29
Hebrews 9:22

WEEK 8
- Exodus 19-20
- Exodus 24-25
- Exodus 26-27
- Exodus 28-29
- Exodus 30-31

MEMORY VERSES:
Exodus 20:1-3
Galatians 5:14

WEEK 9
- Exodus 32-33
- Exodus 34-36:1
- Exodus 40
- Leviticus 8-9
- Leviticus 16-17

MEMORY VERSES:
Exodus 33:16
Matthew 22:37-39

WEEK 10
- ❏ Leviticus 23
- ❏ Leviticus 26
- ❏ Numbers 11-12
- ❏ Numbers 13-14
- ❏ Numbers 16-17

MEMORY VERSES:
Leviticus 26:13
Deuteronomy 31:7-8

WEEK 11
- ❏ Numbers 20; 27:12-23
- ❏ Numbers 34-35
- ❏ Deuteronomy 1-2
- ❏ Deuteronomy 3-4
- ❏ Deuteronomy 6-7

MEMORY VERSES:
Deuteronomy 4:7; 6:4-9

WEEK 12
- ❏ Deuteronomy 8-9
- ❏ Deuteronomy 30-31
- ❏ Deuteronomy 32:48-52; 34
- ❏ Joshua 1-2
- ❏ Joshua 3-4

MEMORY VERSES:
Joshua 1:8-9
Psalm 1:1-2

WEEK 13
- ❏ Joshua 5:10-15; 6
- ❏ Joshua 7-8
- ❏ Joshua 23-24
- ❏ Judges 2-3
- ❏ Judges 4

MEMORY VERSES:
Joshua 24:14-15
Judges 2:12

WEEK 14
- ❏ Judges 6-7
- ❏ Judges 13-14
- ❏ Judges 15-16
- ❏ Ruth 1-2
- ❏ Ruth 3-4

MEMORY VERSES:
Psalm 19:14
Galatians 4:4-5

WEEK 15
- ❏ 1 Samuel 1-2
- ❏ 1 Samuel 3; 8
- ❏ 1 Samuel 9-10
- ❏ 1 Samuel 13-14
- ❏ 1 Samuel 15-16

MEMORY VERSES:
1 Samuel 15:22; 16:7

WEEK 16
- ❏ 1 Samuel 17-18
- ❏ 1 Samuel 19-20
- ❏ 1 Samuel 21-22
- ❏ Psalm 22; 1 Samuel 24-25:1
- ❏ 1 Samuel 28; 31

MEMORY VERSES:
1 Samuel 17:46-47
2 Timothy 4:17a

WEEK 17
- ❏ 2 Samuel 1; 2:1-7
- ❏ 2 Samuel 3:1; 5; Psalm 23
- ❏ 2 Samuel 6-7
- ❏ Psalm 18; 2 Samuel 9
- ❏ 2 Samuel 11-12

MEMORY VERSES:
Psalms 23:1-3; 51:10-13

WEEK 18
- ❏ Psalm 51
- ❏ 2 Samuel 24; Psalm 24
- ❏ Psalm 1; 19
- ❏ Psalms 103; 119:1-48
- ❏ Psalm 119:49-128

MEMORY VERSES:
Psalms 1:1-7; 119:7-11

WEEK 19
- ❏ Psalms 119:129-176; 139
- ❏ Psalms 148-150
- ❏ 1 Kings 2
- ❏ 1 Kings 3; 6
- ❏ 1 Kings 8; 9:1-9

MEMORY VERSES:
Psalms 139:1-3; 139:15-16

WEEK 20
- ❏ Proverbs 1-2
- ❏ Proverbs 3-4
- ❏ Proverbs 16-18
- ❏ Proverbs 31
- ❏ 1 Kings 11-12

MEMORY VERSES:
Proverbs 1:7; 3:5-6

WEEK 21
- ❏ 1 Kings 16:29-34; 17
- ❏ 1 Kings 18-19
- ❏ 1 Kings 21-22
- ❏ 2 Kings 2
- ❏ 2 Kings 5; 6:1-23

MEMORY VERSES:
Psalm 17:15; 63:1

WEEK 22
- ❏ Jonah 1-2
- ❏ Jonah 3-4
- ❏ Hosea 1-3
- ❏ Amos 1:1; 9
- ❏ Joel 1-3

MEMORY VERSES:
Psalm 16:11
John 11:25-26

WEEK 23
- ❏ Isaiah 6; 9
- ❏ Isaiah 44-45
- ❏ Isaiah 52-53
- ❏ Isaiah 65-66
- ❏ Micah 1; 4:6-13; 5

MEMORY VERSES:
Isaiah 53:5-6
1 Peter 2:23-24

WEEK 24
- ❏ 2 Kings 17-18
- ❏ 2 Kings 19-21
- ❏ 2 Kings 22-23
- ❏ Jeremiah 1-3:5
- ❏ Jeremiah 25; 29

MEMORY VERSES:
Proverbs 29:18
Jeremiah 1:15

WEEK 25
- ❏ Jeremiah 31:31-40; 32-33
- ❏ Jeremiah 52; 2 Kings 24-25
- ❏ Ezekiel 1:1-3; 36:16-38; 37
- ❏ Daniel 1-2
- ❏ Daniel 3-4

MEMORY VERSES:
Ezekiel 36:26-27
Daniel 4:35

WEEK 26
- ❏ Daniel 5-6
- ❏ Daniel 9-10; 12
- ❏ Ezra 1-2
- ❏ Ezra 3-4
- ❏ Ezra 5-6

MEMORY VERSES:
Daniel 6:26-27; 9:19

WEEK 27
- ❏ Zechariah 1:1-6; 2; 12
- ❏ Ezra 7-8
- ❏ Ezra 9-10
- ❏ Esther 1-2
- ❏ Esther 3-4

MEMORY VERSES:
Zephaniah 3:17
1 Peter 3:15

WEEK 28
- [ ] Esther 5-7
- [ ] Esther 8-10
- [ ] Nehemiah 1-2
- [ ] Nehemiah 3-4
- [ ] Nehemiah 5-6

MEMORY VERSES:
Deuteronomy 29:29
Psalm 101:3-4

WEEK 29
- [ ] Nehemiah 7-8
- [ ] Nehemiah 9
- [ ] Nehemiah 10
- [ ] Nehemiah 11
- [ ] Nehemiah 12

MEMORY VERSES:
Nehemiah 6:9
Nehemiah 9:6

WEEK 30
- [ ] Nehemiah 13
- [ ] Malachi 1
- [ ] Malachi 2
- [ ] Malachi 3
- [ ] Malachi 4

MEMORY VERSES:
Psalm 51:17
Colossians 1:19-20

WEEK 31
- [ ] Luke 1
- [ ] Luke 2
- [ ] Matthew 1-2
- [ ] Mark 1
- [ ] John 1

MEMORY VERSES:
John 1:1-2, 14

WEEK 32
- [ ] Matthew 3-4
- [ ] Matthew 5
- [ ] Matthew 6
- [ ] Matthew 7
- [ ] Matthew 8

MEMORY VERSES:
Matthew 5:16; 6:33

WEEK 33
- [ ] Luke 9:10-62
- [ ] Mark 9
- [ ] Luke 12
- [ ] John 3-4
- [ ] Luke 14

MEMORY VERSES:
Luke 14:26-27, 33

WEEK 34
- [ ] John 6
- [ ] Matthew 19:16-30
- [ ] Luke 15-16
- [ ] Luke 17:11-37; 18
- [ ] Mark 10

MEMORY VERSES:
Mark 10:45
John 6:37

WEEK 35
- [ ] John 11; Matthew 21:1-13
- [ ] John 13
- [ ] John 14-15
- [ ] John 16
- [ ] Matthew 24:1-31

MEMORY VERSES:
John 13:34-35; 15:4-5

WEEK 36
- [ ] Matthew 24:32-51
- [ ] John 17
- [ ] Matthew 26:47-27:31
- [ ] Matthew 27:32-66; Luke 23:26-56
- [ ] John 19

MEMORY VERSES:
Luke 23:34
John 17:3

WEEK 37
- ☐ Mark 16
- ☐ Luke 24
- ☐ John 20-21
- ☐ Matthew 28
- ☐ Acts 1

MEMORY VERSES:
Matthew 28:18-20
Acts 1:8

WEEK 38
- ☐ Acts 2-3
- ☐ Acts 4-5
- ☐ Acts 6
- ☐ Acts 7
- ☐ Acts 8-9

MEMORY VERSES:
Acts 2:42; 4:31

WEEK 39
- ☐ Acts 10-11
- ☐ Acts 12
- ☐ Acts 13-14
- ☐ James 1-2
- ☐ James 3-5

MEMORY VERSES:
James 1:2-4; 2:17

WEEK 40
- ☐ Acts 15-16
- ☐ Galatians 1-3
- ☐ Galatians 4-6
- ☐ Acts 17-18:17
- ☐ 1 Thessalonians 1-2

MEMORY VERSES:
Acts 17:11, 24-25

WEEK 41
- ☐ 1 Thessalonians 3-5
- ☐ 2 Thessalonians 1-3
- ☐ Acts 18:18-28; 19
- ☐ 1 Corinthians 1-2
- ☐ 1 Corinthians 3-4

MEMORY VERSES:
1 Corinthians 1:18
1 Thessalonians 5:23-24

WEEK 42
- ☐ 1 Corinthians 5-6
- ☐ 1 Corinthians 7-8
- ☐ 1 Corinthians 9-10
- ☐ 1 Corinthians 11-12
- ☐ 1 Corinthians 13-14

MEMORY VERSES:
1 Corinthians 10:13; 13:13

WEEK 43
- ☐ 1 Corinthians 15-16
- ☐ 2 Corinthians 1-2
- ☐ 2 Corinthians 3-4
- ☐ 2 Corinthians 5-6
- ☐ 2 Corinthians 7-8

MEMORY VERSES:
Romans 1:16-17
1 Corinthians 15:3-4

WEEK 44
- ☐ 2 Corinthians 9-10
- ☐ 2 Corinthians 11-13
- ☐ Romans 1-2; Acts 20:1-3
- ☐ Romans 3-4
- ☐ Romans 5-6

MEMORY VERSES:
Romans 5:1
2 Corinthians 10:4

WEEK 45
- ☐ Romans 7-8
- ☐ Romans 9-10
- ☐ Romans 11-12
- ☐ Romans 13-14
- ☐ Romans 15-16

MEMORY VERSES:
Romans 8:1; 12:1-2

WEEK 46
- ❏ Acts 20-21
- ❏ Acts 22-23
- ❏ Acts 24-25
- ❏ Acts 26-27
- ❏ Acts 28

MEMORY VERSES:
Acts 20:24
2 Corinthians 4:7-10

WEEK 47
- ❏ Colossians 1-2
- ❏ Colossians 3-4
- ❏ Ephesians 1-2
- ❏ Ephesians 3-4
- ❏ Ephesians 5-6

MEMORY VERSES:
Ephesians 2:8-10
Colossians 2:6-7

WEEK 48
- ❏ Philippians 1-2
- ❏ Philippians 3-4
- ❏ Hebrews 1-2
- ❏ Hebrews 3-4
- ❏ Hebrews 5-6

MEMORY VERSES:
Philippians 3:7-8
Hebrews 4:14-16

WEEK 49
- ❏ Hebrews 7
- ❏ Hebrews 8-9
- ❏ Hebrews 10
- ❏ Hebrews 11
- ❏ Hebrews 12

MEMORY VERSES:
Galatians 2:19-20
2 Corinthians 5:17

WEEK 50
- ❏ 1 Timothy 1-3
- ❏ 1 Timothy 4-6
- ❏ 2 Timothy 1-2
- ❏ 2 Timothy 3-4
- ❏ 1 Peter 1-2

MEMORY VERSES:
2 Timothy 2:1-2, 15

WEEK 51
- ❏ 1 Peter 3-4
- ❏ 1 Peter 5; 2 Peter 1
- ❏ 2 Peter 2-3
- ❏ 1 John 1-3
- ❏ 1 John 4-5

MEMORY VERSES:
1 Peter 2:11
1 John 4:10-11

WEEK 52
- ❏ Revelation 1
- ❏ Revelation 2-3
- ❏ Revelation 4-5
- ❏ Revelation 18-19
- ❏ Revelation 20-22

MEMORY VERSES:
Revelation 3:19; 21:3-4

Leader's Guide & Bonus Content

Visit **https://biblestudy.tips/workbook-bonuses** to download the Leader's Guide and additional bonus content for this workbook.

Bonus content includes:

- Printable worksheets

- Reading plans

- Logos Bible software workflows

- Additional resources

Bible Software Deals

One of the best ways to get the most out of the BibleStudy.Tips workbook is to utilize its methods with Bible software.

To help you build your digital Bible software library we have partnered with both Olive Tree Bible Software and Logos Bible Software. Visit the links below to access their offers.

Olive Tree Bible Software
https://biblestudy.tips/workbook-olivetree-offer

This link includes several of our recommended resources, along with some additional Bible study tools worth adding to your library.

Use the coupon code **BST10** to save 10% on your order.

Logos Bible Software
https://biblestudy.tips/workbook-logos-offer

The Logos Fundamentals package is a complete Bible study library for under $100. It includes over 50 trustworthy titles that will help you study God's Word.

BibleStudy.Tips Workshop

Do you need a more hands on approach to this workbook? Do you want me to teach these Bible study methods at your church or school? If so, then book a BibleStudy.Tips workshop and I will host an in-person or virtual training session to your group.

Visit **https://biblestudy.tips/workshop** to contact us and learn more.

Acknowledgements

With any book, there are always so many people to thank. A work like this does not happen in a vacuum. First, I want to thank our Lord, Jesus Christ. Without being raised to life and knowing there is a blessed hope, this book would be meaningless. I am grateful for the passion you have given me for your Word and the desire to see others learn it, connect with you, and grow in their faith experience.

Jaimie, BibleStudy.Tips and this workbook would not be possible without your continual love and support. You believe in me when no one else does and you always push me to reach for my dreams. This book happened because of your friendship and sacrifice.

Mom & Dad, thank you for your love and raising me in the Faith. You always tell me I can do great things, and I believe this work is a testament to our family's legacy in the gospel, going all the way back to great-great-grandpa Eldridge Staten.

Pastor Miles, thank you for the wonderful preface and the faith you put in a guy like me to share God's Word with your flock. I am forever grateful for my time at Redemption Spokane and for the friendship we forged.

BibleStudy.Tips family, this book & ministry would not exist without you, your support, and continual feedback. This book is for you.

Robby Gallaty & the Replicate team, thank you for your mentorship these past years. Thanks for letting me add to your journaling method & for use of the F-260 reading plan. I pray this resource helps make stronger disciples!

Coby Munsey, you're a real one. Thank you for your support & friendship all these years.

Harold Coleman, you've been a great friend & coworker. Thanks for pouring into me all these years and for all the walks to Starbucks. You kept pushing me forward.

You, the person holding this book. Thank you for giving me a chance by picking up this book. I wrote this for you & everyone you'll share it with. I am eternally grateful for you & I pray this book blesses your life beyond measure.

Bible Study Tips on YouTube

Want more Bible study tips? Check out the BibleStudy.Tips YouTube channel for tips, tricks, and live Bible studies at **YouTube.com/BibleStudyTips**

Bibliography

Fuhr, Richard Alan, and Andreas J. Köstenberger. *Inductive Bible Study: Observation, Interpretation, and Application through the Lenses of History, Literature, and Theology*. B & H Academic, 2016.

Saxton, David W. *God's Battle Plan for the Mind: the Puritan Practice of Biblical Meditation*. Reformation Heritage Books, 2015.

About the Author

LaRosa Johnson is a Bible teacher, technologist, and fitness coach. He resides in Jacksonville, North Carolina with his wife and children. He's a regular guy with no formal qualifications or theological degrees whose curiosity has driven him to learn more about the Bible. Some might describe him as having a bent toward pastoring and teaching, but it so happens that he simply enjoys adding value to the lives of others through what he learns from the Bible.

Years of personal spiritual development have given LaRosa a genuine love for Bible study. The Lord put him on this earth to share that love for Bible study with others. Over the years this has taken many forms, whether it be teaching, writing, or producing online courses.

At the end of the day, LaRosa's desire is to play his part in fulfilling the Great Commission by making disciples who are equipped to make disciples by caring for them both spiritually and physically.